INCREDIBLE BEAR ATTACKS

INCREDIBLE BEAR ATTACKS

*Terrifying Tales of Savage Encounters
between Bears and People*

EDITED BY LAMAR UNDERWOOD

LYONS
PRESS

Essex, Connecticut

An imprint of The Globe Pequot Publishing Group, Inc.
64 South Main Street
Essex, CT 06426
www.globepequot.com

Distributed by NATIONAL BOOK NETWORK

British Library Cataloguing in Publication Information available

Library of Congress Cataloging-in-Publication Data Available

ISBN 9781493085248 (paperback) | ISBN 9781493085255 (epub)

♾™ The paper used in this publication meets the minimum requirements of American National Standard for Information Sciences—Permanence of Paper for Printed Library Materials, ANSI/ NISO Z39.48-1992.

Contents

PREFACE

Our fate! Shakespeare, in Hamlet, described it as "the slings and arrows of outrageous fortune."

Is "outrageous fortune" waiting to strike us? Can it be avoided?

Charles Lindbergh, renowned aviator, said, "Everything is chance. You can guard against the high percentage of chance but not against chance itself."

Experienced and famous pilot Ernest K. Gann titled his memoir *Fate Is the Hunter*.

From the first chapter in this book until the last, you are going to hear about people who inadvertently gambled with their lives in bear country—sometimes vast wilderness regions, sometimes pockets of wilderness hanging on at the edges of civilization.

The call of wild places is irresistible. Hiking, camping, fishing, photography. These activities conjure up images of enjoying life in places far removed from the crushing chains of cities and suburbs. These places are also the homes of the biggest, most potentially dangerous and unpredictable creatures to walk the earth. Bears!

Trails, campsites, creek and river pools, vistas overlooking pure and uncut forests—any of these destinations could be occupied when you arrive. And because bears are great wanderers of the forest, even after you've set up your tent, or cleaned fish, or prepared a meal, you might have an unwelcome visitor.

What now?

In the pages of this book, you are going to share the terrifying and unexpected collisions between humans and bears. Such real-life episodes have many endings, none of which are a sure thing no matter what you do. Sometimes your noisemaking and antics can make a bear go away. Sometimes they don't go away.

Reading about the experiences of others in navigating bear country will arm you with tips and skills that might save your life—or keep you from being arrested. Carrying firearms in Yellowstone and other places where they are prohibited can put you in jail. Even worse, shooting a bear simply because it is crossing your path will take a lot of explaining to keep you from mug shots and finger-printing. You're going to need a good lawyer after you're thinking, "There's a bear. I'd better shoot it."

While no one is going to put you in the slammer for shooting a bear that's trying to bite your face off, you'd better have good proof of your predicament. And the whole subject of firearms for bear protection needs, and gets, a lot of study and opinions in print and social media. How about a pump shotgun with five loads of buckshot? I've seen it carried on canoe trips in remote bear haunts. For backpacking, the biggest, meanest magnum revolver carried in a holster is a common choice.

The holster subject jumps straight out of the firearms debate into carrying the legal and most-widely used bear protection device: bear spray. If you're going to carry bear spray—and the overwhelming opinion is that you should—two questions remain: *How* will you carry it? *Where* will you carry it?

If you round a bend in the trail and suddenly find yourself face-to-face with a grizzly or black bear, you'll want to get the spray into action immediately, if not sooner. There will be no time for fumbling with zippers or snaps to open packs or pouches where your bear spray has been comfortably residing.

Waist and shoulder holsters that keep your bear spray within quick-draw reach are readily available. The fast-draw skills of western movie heroes, like Shane against Jack Wilson, come to mind. They could be useful in a head-on collision with a bear.

Packs of information on bear spray and holsters and carry devices are readily available on the internet. You can even watch videos that show the spray in action. You'll see it shooting out in a misty cloud at various ranges. It's only practice, of course, without a real bear. But you'll get the idea.

The story that begins this book is, to me, the most gut-wrenching of all bear attack stories. It reminds me of watching a horror movie with your mind screaming, "Don't open that door!"

This happened before the wide use of bear spray in a great American treasure: Yellowstone Park. A vibrant, intelligent young woman, experienced in backpacking, flew there from Switzerland, following her dreams of camping in the Yellowstone backcountry. She carefully followed every rule and talked with the park rangers. Her campsite was flawless. Food bags were hanging from a tree, yards from her tent. Before zipping up her sleeping bag, she made a note in her trail diary: "I have taken all precautions."

She was wrong. She had ignored a solid warning from the park rangers: "It is dangerous to travel alone—take extra precautions."

Now, fate was ready to play its hand.

And it did!

Welcome to bear country. Out here, what you don't know can kill you.

CHAPTER ONE

Horror in Yellowstone

Kathleen Snow

(Excerpted from Taken by Bear in Yellowstone, *Lyons Press, 2016.)*

ON HORSEBACK, A YELLOWSTONE PARK RANGER WAS SEARCHING FOR A missing hiker. As he approached a campsite and tent, his horse suddenly spooked. Something about the ground ahead was frightening to the animal. The ranger walked to the tent and saw rip marks in the tent fly near the door. The tent was empty. A tragedy was coming to light.

National Park Service—Yellowstone
Case Incident Record Number: 842913
Location: Backcountry Site 5W1, White Lake
Date/Time: Monday, July 30, 1984, 11:00 p.m.

Brigitta Fredenhagen had never been to Yellowstone Park before. She hoped to experience its natural web of life by hiking and camping in its beautiful (but wild) backcountry. Brigitta's Yellowstone journey began on July 25, 1984, when she boarded an airplane from Paris to New York City. Her birthplace and residence was Basel, a Swiss city on the Rhine River, home of pharmaceutical companies and the annual Art Basel, one of the world's most prestigious art shows. Brigitta, her brother, and sister-in-law were all from Switzerland. She had educated herself about Yellowstone and carried a hiking guide. She attached to her backpack two "bear bells," whose ringing could warn bears of her approach on the trail. A Board of Inquiry later found that she "had apparently received and followed all safety recommendations."

That morning, a Monday, July 30, 1984, Brigitta, her brother, and sister-in-law arrived at the Pelican Valley Trailhead at 11:00 a.m. That night a thunderstorm would boom and flash, but for now Brigitta saw sun and wildflowers, smelled wild mint and pine. From the trailhead, the three hiked 3.3 miles to the Pelican

Creek Bridge, and then another 2.5 miles to the Astringent Creek Bridge. Brigitta settled into the rhythm of her lug-sole boots—size 5½—striking dirt, feeling the strength of her legs, conditioned by many other hikes and backpacks, for she was an experienced outdoorswoman.

That night, alone, she would set up her tent in Backcountry Site 5W1 at White Lake. But it was still day, and she felt the security of her brother and sister-in-law hiking alongside her. She carried a pale-green paperback, *Yellowstone Trails*, by Yellowstone Lake District ranger Mark C. Marschall. After Brigitta disappeared, Ranger Marschall was one of the park personnel to join the search for her. His guidebook notes:

> The trails in the Pelican Valley area should be especially attractive to those hikers interested in viewing wildlife. But if the thought of viewing a grizzly bear isn't especially attractive to you, then maybe you should consider a different area. Grizzly bears are drawn to Pelican Valley for its relatively lush plant growth of grasses, sedges and forbs. Sightings aren't uncommon, though encounters between bear and people are rare.

On the far side of the Astringent Creek Bridge, as at so many junctures, Brigitta made a choice that may have determined her fate. As she had planned, there where the Astringent Creek–Broad Creek Trail started northward, she chose to hike north alone.

She turned to her brother and sister-in-law and said goodbye. She watched them hike back toward the Pelican Valley Trailhead and their rented car, because unlike her—as they explained the next day, July 31, to Lake District ranger Timothy P. Blank—they had not brought their backpacking gear with them. From that point on, Brigitta would be hiking—and planned to camp tonight at the site she had registered for, near Broad Creek—alone.

She was a colorful figure on the trail, her red backpack carrying all that she needed to camp overnight. Her food supplies—a comforting thought—included "instant noodles, smoked ham in a plastic sack, dried peaches, two slices of bread, two granola bars, tea leaves, powdered milk, cereal, and liquid tea in a metal container." She wore leather boots with sturdy Vibram soles, blue-beige jeans, brown jacket, and a yellow and gray blouse. She saw much beauty along the way and recorded it with her 35 mm camera and lens; the film was later found and developed.

Among the meadows and the lodgepole-pine forest with spruce understory, Brigitta must have seen an orange placard indicating the campsite. Brigitta did not know the history of White Lake Campsite. At the end of the day, Brigitta focused the lens on her cookstove set up in the fire ring fifty feet from her tent, and made a final exposure.

* * *

[Editor's Note: At this point in her narrative, Kathleen Snow gives readers more information about the beginning on the trip.]

On July 29, Brigitta's family group drove to the Grand Canyon of the Yellowstone—twenty miles long and fifteen hundred feet deep—admiring the lower falls' plunging water and sprays of mist. Then, by herself—to obtain a backcountry camping permit for the following day—Brigitta walked into the Canyon Ranger Station.

What happened next is narrated in the Case Incident Record by the park professionals who were directly involved.

"[A]t approximately 12:15 p.m. a young lady entered the office area and began looking at a large Yellowstone topographical map, which is mounted on the east wall of the Canyon Ranger Station Office," reported Law Enforcement Specialist Floyd Klang, after interviewing Ranger James G. Youngblood on July 31.

Youngblood was on duty at the ranger station and helped Brigitta with her backcountry permit. Ranger Youngblood described the young lady as pretty, 5'3" to 5'5" tall, 120 pounds, dark, wavy shoulder length hair, wearing blue jeans and a knit pullover shirt or blouse . . . he handed Ms. Fredenhagen a preassembled package of backcountry informational brochures . . . Youngblood called the backcountry office, located at Mammoth, and received a confirmation to issue Ms. Fredenhagen a backcountry campsite permit for site 5-B-1, for the night of July 30, 1984. The number of this permit was designated as 847N806.

The trail that Ms. Fredenhagen planned to use is commonly known as the Astringent–Broad Creek Trail and she was planning on beginning her hike at a trailhead in Pelican Valley, located approximately 3 miles east of Fishing Bridge. Ranger Youngblood . . . wrote the following information on the backcountry permit: Broad Creek, Bears, Firearms, H20, Food, Fires . . . he gave Ms. Fredenhagen verbal information, including the following:

"The bears in Yellowstone National Park are dangerous, that she should not attempt to approach them, she should hang her foodstuffs in a tree and well away from the campsite area, don't have any foods or foodstuffs near the tent or sleeping equipment and generally keep a clean camp . . . It is dangerous to travel alone—take extra precautions, if she should get hurt, like breaking a leg one might be in big trouble."

Ms. Fredenhagen asked questions concerning locating the campsite and the trail. Ranger Youngblood advised Ms. Fredenhagen that the trail was marked with a sign with the campsite number printed on it.

Ranger Youngblood stated that Ms. Fredenhagen appeared to be very intelligent, that she spoke near perfect English and that she did not appear to have any difficulty in communicating with him.

Brigitta had now obtained the necessary permit to camp the night of July 30 at the remote Backcountry Site 5B1, at Broad Creek. After her overnight camp alone, she would hike the connecting Wapiti Lake Trail to Canyon, where she would rejoin her brother and sister-in-law at the Grand Canyon of the Yellowstone.

That night, July 29, Brigitta, her brother, and sister-in-law slept in the public campground near Norris Geyser Basin, where hot springs spread acres of greens, blues, and yellows, as vivid as dreams. Tomorrow they would hike into the wilder world of Yellowstone's backcountry.

The next morning, to begin their hike, the three Swiss visitors drove past Fishing Bridge toward Pelican Valley. Pelicans could be seen on Yellowstone Lake, near where the three parked their car. Just past Indian Pond, and four miles north of the islet called Pelican Roost, the Pelican Valley Trail began.

At 11:00 a.m., with two "bear bells" on her pack, Brigitta signed the trail register where, in International Orange, a new placard read: "Warning—Grizzly Frequenting Area Traversed by This Trail, Be Alert."

In fact, grizzlies sometimes traveled on human trails—the paths of least resistance—especially in the seldom used (by humans) evenings, nights, and dawns. Brigitta, her brother, and sister-in-law followed the trail for two miles, emerging into the broad expanse of Pelican Valley.

"The area is ideal grizzly habitat and you will probably spot several droppings and diggings along the way," warned writer Orville E. Bach Jr. in the 1979 edition of his book *Hiking the Yellowstone Backcountry*, a book Brigitta may have read. Bach advised the following:

> Make noise and remain alert as you traverse the valley. Coyotes are frequently sighted throughout the valley searching for small game. At the 3 mile point you reach Pelican Creek and a junction with the old fire road used to provide access to forest fire areas. Pelican Creek moves along rather slowly. The water is not very cold and therefore makes poor drinking water.

Brigitta told her brother and sister-in-law that she might not make it all the way to 5B1. That afternoon Brigitta made two significant choices. First, at 5.8 miles from the Pelican Valley Trailhead, past the Astringent Creek Bridge, she chose to hike on alone.

Second, she stopped for the night at a backcountry campsite that was not the campsite she had registered for, but one that was nearer. Brigitta had registered for Campsite 5B1 at Broad Creek, but 5B1 was an additional 3.5 miles [described alternatively in the Case Incident Record as 4.5 miles] beyond where she ended up camping [White Lake campsite 5W1]. Did she stop short of her assigned campsite because she felt anxious about proceeding farther into the backcountry? In the Case Incident Record, Ranger Blank noted that Brigitta "expressed a concern about meeting animals and about getting back on time. [She] decided to change [her] itinerary and return to the Pelican Trailhead most likely by the Pelican Creek Trail"; whatever was going through Brigitta's mind, she continued on while her brother and sister-in-law returned to the Pelican Valley Trailhead. Evidence later indicated that Brigitta hiked north up the Astringent Creek–Broad Creek Trail. She took 5W1.

In 1982, from July 19 through July 26, the site received "Strong Bear Warnings" for reported heavy bear activity, as did all of Pelican Valley. From July 26 through August 2, 1982, "Strong Bear Warnings" were issued for Campsite 5W1 alone. But in 1983, no warnings were issued.

Now, on July 30, 1984, standing by herself at Campsite 5W1, Brigitta photographed the arm of White Lake on her right, the center of the shot showing a lone sapling.

Perhaps Brigitta looked at campsite 5W1 and decided that she was too tired, or had had enough, or was feeling too lonely to go on to her assigned campsite. For reasons known only to herself, she chose to stay the night at 5W1.

In another twist of fate, Brigitta should not have been alone at 5W1. A party of three hikers had registered for the campsite that night, but they didn't start hiking until 6:00 p.m., too late to reach 5W1, so they camped in lower Pelican Valley instead.

Brigitta's next-to-last photograph was described by a ranger as "Looking from meadow SSW of tent. Campfire ring left center of photo." It showed the path leading directly to 5W1, where among the evergreens Brigitta later planted her green-domed tent.

Brigitta's final photograph showed her cookstove set up in the fire ring fifty feet from her tent. The shadows in the photo suggested she took this frame at approximately 5:30 p.m. (plus or minus an hour). She heated and ate her dinner (perhaps ham, since five slices were later found) and then drank tea while the sun slipped behind the treetops. Clouds began rolling in, suggesting rain later in the night.

To cache her food from animals, Brigitta located two old lodgepole pines with low broken limbs eighty-five feet east of her campsite. She climbed the ladder-like limbs to a height of twelve feet and suspended parachute cord between the two trees, from which she hung her food, cook kit, and stove. By then the evening light was nearly gone. She probably felt physically tired, but with the tiredness came the hiked-out calm that is one of the rewards of backpacking.

Her legs tingled, even ached, and she pulled her red mummy-shaped sleeping bag from its stuff sack, fluffed it up, then laid it inside her tent, headfirst toward the tent door. She put on garments to sleep in, and wrapped the clothes she had hiked in and probably cooked in within a plastic bag folded inside her poncho. On her right side she set her flashlight, and on her left side, her cassette-tape music player. She probably sat on top of her sleeping bag, legs crossed, to write in her journal. Among other notes about the day, she wrote: "I have taken all precautions."

Finally she crawled into her sleeping bag, her feet toward the rear of the tent, her head near the front with its zippered door: her only exit. She wore blue cotton pajamas, socks, and a sweater. It may have taken awhile, in the backcountry of Yellowstone far from home, but presumably she fell asleep. During the night a lightning-laced thunderstorm moved in. Perhaps Brigitta briefly awakened. But she had stretched a waterproof rainfly tightly above her tent and remained dry inside her personal cocoon. The only sounds she could probably hear were the thunderclaps overhead and the rain hitting her tent. Listening to the rain, she probably fell asleep again.

* * *

On Tuesday, July 31, at the Pelican Valley Trailhead, Brigitta's brother and sister-in-law expected to see her hiking toward them, a smile on her face. It was 3:30 p.m., the agreed upon time. Brigitta, normally a punctual person, did not appear. After half an hour, anxiety set in. An hour passed. Then another. Now their fear was sharp.

Around 6:00 p.m. Brigitta's brother hurried to the Fishing Bridge Visitor Center to report Brigitta overdue. Park Naturalist Lori Qualman called Ranger Marschall. "I asked [the brother] to return to the trailhead and continue waiting for his sister for another hour," Marschall stated in his park report:

> I attempted to contact by radio Ranger Bill Berg who was in Pelican Springs Patrol Cabin that evening. I was called to a fire alarm at the Lake Lodge before I could reach him. When I returned to the Ranger Station, at about [8:00 p.m.], [the brother] was there and told me his sister had still not returned to the trailhead. I continued to try and contact Ranger Berg via radio while I asked [the brother] questions about his sister and her trip.

Using the brother's information, Ranger Marschall wrote an "Attempt to Locate" and contacted the Yellowstone Communications Center to have it read over the park's internal radio frequency. The operator's urgent voice, "Missing Hiker in Pelican Valley: Name Brigitta Fredenhagen," was heard by Park Service personnel across both Yellowstone's developed area and backcountry.

As it turned out, Brigitta was not the only missing person that day. A search party headed by Incident Commander Randy King was moving south from Specimen Ridge toward Broad Creek (where Brigitta was registered to camp), looking for another missing hiker. Brigitta's "Attempt to Locate" was transmitted to this search party as well.

At 8:00 p.m. Brigitta's brother and sister-in-law met with Lake District ranger David Spirtes at Lake Ranger Station, telling him "that Brigitta, who was very responsible and punctual, was now 4 1⁄2 hours overdue."

"I finally contacted Bill Berg [by radio] at approximately [8:14 p.m.]," Ranger Marschall wrote. Ranger Berg was known to be staying at the Pelican Springs Patrol Cabin in Pelican Valley that evening. Marschall then alerted Berg to the missing Brigitta:

> I gave him a description of Brigitta and asked Berg to go out into the valley and see if he could see any sign of her. I told Berg not to search after dark. Berg checked back in at approximately [9:30 p.m.] and said he had seen no sign of hikers.
>
> From approximately [8:30 to 9:30 p.m.] the Pelican [Valley] trailhead was monitored by either [name withheld] or [the brother and sister-in-law, who] decided to go back to Norris and camp for the evening. I had them leave a note for Brigitta at the

trailhead register telling her to call our emergency phone number if she arrived late. I had Ranger Steve Harrel check the trailhead hourly from [10:00 p.m. to 3:00 a.m.] that night.

Brigitta did not return to the trailhead that night.

* * *

On Wednesday, August 1, Brigitta was still missing, perhaps lying injured in the remote backcountry. Her brother and sister-in-law were "extremely concerned." Writing in his later report, Lake District ranger David Spirtes noted the following:

At approximately [9:00 a.m.] on August 1, [her brother and sister-in-law] returned from Norris Campground to the Lake Ranger Station. I advised them that a ranger was on the way into Brigitta's campsite and the best thing that they could do was to wait at the trailhead and to let us know immediately if she returned. I assured them that we would contact them at the trailhead as soon as we had any news.

Following Ranger Spirtes' advice, Brigitta's brother and sister-in-law went back to the trailhead and waited. They strained to see movement coming toward them, movement of any kind that might indicate Brigitta coming home.

Early that morning, looking for Brigitta, Ranger Marschall rode on horseback toward campsite 5B1 on Broad Creek, the campsite she had registered for. His report detailed his efforts to find her:

I checked the area downstream from Pelican Bridge and the area north of Astringent Creek Junction but otherwise I rode up the Astringent Creek–Broad Creek trail headed for Brigitta's proposed campsite of 5B1. At approximately [8:30 a.m.] I talked with hiker [name withheld] near the Astringent Creek Junction. He reported seeing a large grizzly bear approximately 15 minutes earlier coming from the Astringent Creek trail area and headed south into Pelican Valley.

At approximately [11:20 a.m.] I arrived at campsite 5W1 on the edge of White Lake. I saw a green dome tent standing and a sleeping bag laid out in front of the tent. As I rode towards the tent, my horse spooked and would approach no closer than 20 yards.

I walked to the tent and saw rip marks in the tent fly near the door. I looked into the tent and saw a sleeping pad, parka, and gear all apparently undisturbed. When I looked around outside the tent I noticed a piece of scalp and hair and a piece of what was apparently muscle tissue.

I immediately called Lake Ranger Station on the radio and notified Area Ranger David Spirtes [now the operations chief and primary investigator] and District Ranger Tim Blank [now the incident commander] of what I had found. While they arranged for a helicopter transport to the scene, I checked the woods to the east of the campsite looking for Brigitta.

I found Brigitta's food cache lying on the ground where it had apparently been ripped apart by a bear. I looked for Brigitta for about 20 minutes, but could not locate her.

Possible human tissue had been found outside of Brigitta's tent. The Park Service response was immediate. "District Ranger Tim

Blank and I got two shotguns, a high-powered rifle, emergency medical technician kit, compass, maps, ammunition, 35mm camera, binoculars, and other emergency equipment and proceeded to the Fishing Bridge helispot," reported Operations Chief Spirtes. He described what he saw:

At [11:58 a.m.] we lifted off en route to White Lake. From the air we observed a green dome tent with Ranger Marschall standing in a meadow, waving his arms, and indicating a landing spot. At [12:06 p.m.], the helicopter touched down. Rangers Marschall and Blank loaded shotguns while I carried the rifle. We began a hasty search of the area.

The dome tent looked normal except for the fresh tear next to the front flap. Six feet away was a zipped-up sleeping bag, appearing as if it had been laid out in the sun. Several feet from the sleeping bag was a piece of lip, and nearby a piece of scalp with hair attached.

Marschall showed us the area, 30 yards to the east, where a bear had apparently gotten her food cache from between two trees. Over the past two days, there had been numerous localized severe thunderstorms pass through the park. Since no trail was discernible, we began a hasty search of the nearby woods.

From the sleeping bag, a trail of tissue led in a northerly direction, including a small piece of scalp, lip, more scalp, a small piece of fat globule, and some shreds of blue cloth. Approximately 22 feet northwest of the tent was an oblong 18-inch by 37-inch patch of discolored grass. Small blue-cloth fibers and tissue could be seen there. In subsequent days the patch smelled, felt greasy, and became more noticeable. It appeared that substantial bleeding took place at this location. This, coupled with the tissue spread around the area, would probably indicate the site where the victim died.

From there a barely discernible trail that went to the east of the fire ring crossed the trail, and went uphill toward the wood in a northeasterly direction was followed. Roughly halfway between the fire ring and final resting place of the body, a bloody sweater with numerous rips and tears was left behind. Thirty feet from where the body was found was a discolored cotton pullover shirt.

The body was lying approximately 250 feet from the tent. It was stretched out prone with the left arm bent at the elbow and pinned under the body. The right arm was extended over the head. Her right foot was detached at the ankle, but laying adjacent to it. Next to her left foot was her stretched-out blue pajama bottoms. . . . The skin on the arms was peeled back as if cased; a characteristic suggestive of the way a grizzly often feeds on a carcass. The body was not eviscerated, although most of the muscle, flesh, and skin was gone from the arms, legs, buttocks, and upper torso.

It was not possible to determine the time of death. . . . The average person after hiking 8.5 miles would eat dinner after arriving at their campsite. . . . The victim's stomach was empty at the autopsy; since it takes approximately 6 hours for food to clear the stomach, this would place the time of death after [10:30 p.m.] if she ate dinner. . . . The rain destroyed much evidence. There was not a single bear hair stuck in the bark or sap of the lodgepole pine that the bear had climbed. The lack of even coagulated globules of blood suggest that it rained during or soon after the victim started bleeding. One had to get down on hands and knees to follow the path where the body had been dragged.

There were only four bear tracks discovered near the site. . . . One scat was discovered at the site and another 1 mile south of the site that contained large pieces of undigested human tissue. Since a bear would normally pass feces from between 12 [and] 48 hours after the time of ingestion of food, it appears that the bear stayed in or returned to the area for at least 12 hours. Two other scats with human remains, one on the trail by the Broad– Pelican Trail Cutoff and a second found on a small pond north of the Mud Kettles, indicate that the bear moved several miles north and several miles east in the day following the killing.

A scat with human remains on top of fresh bear tracks that measured 5½ by 4¾ inches for the front pad and 4¾ by 8 inches for the rear, was dropped on the afternoon or evening of August 2 or the morning of August 3. This scat was nearly 10% human and contained a large quantity of hair. Given the normal digestive time for a bear, this suggests that the bear returned to feed on the second day, July 31. The one measurable track found at 5W1 was on top of fresh rained-on ground and would seem to verify this. These scats with human remains also contained elk hair and no maggot casings, which in the end of July indicate a successful predatory bear.

Teeth marks that seemed to correspond to a matching set of canine teeth were measured on Fredenhagen's left hand at 5.5 cm and on the left shoulder at 5.3 cm. These correspond to the measurement of teeth marks recovered from an aluminum cookpot. The dental impression left in the cooking pot remains the best piece of evidence to identify the individual bear. . . .

At approximately [5:50 p.m.], Fredenhagen's body and belongings were flown back to Fishing Bridge. Incident Commander Timothy

Blank wrote that "After the body was found, [names withheld] went to the trailhead and informed the brother and sister-in-law and provided support." Blank detailed the Park Service's concern for the relatives:

> They took [brother and sister-in-law] to their house and stayed with them for the afternoon and arranged for lodging and meals at Lake. At [6:00 p.m.], Ranger Blank met with them and told them what had happened, arranged for medication for the sister-in-law and assisted the brother in contacting his father in Switzerland and making arrangements for them to fly to Switzerland. Arrangements were made with the mortuary and the hospital for the body and the coroner's report.
>
> On August 2, Ranger Blank spent most of the day with the brother and sister-in-law, making arrangements for airline flights, car rental return, cremation of Brigitta's remains, and security arrangements with airport personnel. Brigitta's belongings were sorted and packed by her brother and sister-in-law.

As Incident Commander Blank reported, "On August 3, the brother and sister-in-law drove to Billings, and on August 4, they flew from Billings to Switzerland with the deceased's ashes."

* * *

Grizzly bear tracks, bite marks, and biological samples can provide forensic proof in investigations of bear attacks. To determine which bear was responsible, on Wednesday, August 1, rangers began field investigation patrols, including night-long patrols, to locate all bears in the area, and trap or tranquilize them. Culvert-pipe bear traps and tracking by both humans and scent dogs were used in an attempt to capture and identify the responsible grizzly.

On Thursday, August 2, rangers spotted Bear #1, a grizzly. In days to come they sighted three more grizzlies (one with a cub), which Marschall noted on his page titled "Bear Descriptions."

Bear #1 Description: 400 lbs, dark wide head, blonde white muzzle, dark rump. Silver tipping on neck and ribs—lightest towards front and gets darker towards rear.

Bear #3[*sic*] Description: Sub-adult grizzly, 150–200 lbs., blonde face, blonde fore-shoulders, blonde ribs. Dark rump and hump.

Bear #4 Description: Sub-adult grizzly. Darker and larger than #3. 200–250 lbs. Silver tipping on ribs, and fore-shoulders, and outside of eyes and on muzzle. Diagonal, elliptical patch of silver tipped fur just behind right shoulder. Visible only in bright light.

Sow and Cub Description: (Sow)—450 lb. grizzly with blonde or silver tipped patch of fur between eyes and nose. Very prominent dark hump and dark rump. Overall appearance dark. Ear tags in both ears. Description: (Cub)—50 lb. grizzly with blonde ribs and collar. Light overall appearance.

Culvert bear traps were flown in by helicopter, baited and set (with rangers safely monitoring them from inside an extra culvert trap through the night). But for the moment all the bears eluded capture.

On Friday, August 3, Marschall noted among other items that "Tracks C followed in towards Pelican TH from about 1 mile out.

Tracks were probably made the night of 8/2/84. Scat #8 picked up on tracks. Scat later tested out positive."

For ten more days, to Monday, August 13, trapping and patrolling continued. Suddenly on August 13 there was a possible suspect. Marschall noted that park personnel "Discovered bear-caused damage in Fishing Bridge campground from approximately 11:00 p.m. the night before. Three (3) traps set in Fishing Bridge campground. All night patrols continue. From Monday, August 13, through Saturday, August 18, Pelican Valley was monitored by rangers to enforce closures and monitor bear activity."

"The bear involved [in Brigitta's death] was never identified or captured despite major efforts," Stephen Herrero wrote one year later in 1985s *Bear Attacks: Their Causes and Avoidance*. "Dr. Meagher [Mary, a Yellowstone research biologist] used available evidence to conclude that the bear was probably a sub-adult grizzly (young grizzlies are more likely to climb trees), probably male, and apparently 'not a naïve bear relative to developed areas and human activities.'"

On August 23, 1984, in the Superintendent's Conference Room at Mammoth Hot Springs, the Board of Inquiry reviewed the facts of Brigitta's death. It reached the following conclusions:

> Based on all available information, the Board found that Brigitta Fredenhagen died as a result of hemorrhage and shock due to multiple wounds inflicted by a single subadult (2–3 years of age) grizzly bear [determined as most probable by park biologist Mary Meagher, based upon data including the size of paw tracks and the size and span of toothmarks].

Ms. Fredenhagen had apparently received and followed all safety recommendations.

As this author can attest, it is natural that women want to participate in the natural world—to hike, to camp, to be free. And it is an entirely different experience to hike companionably with others than to do so by yourself. At its best, experiencing nature when you are alone can be a spiritual, even transcendent human experience.

Perhaps Brigitta was hoping to have that kind of experience. Brigitta was found to have done nothing wrong.

Being a bear, the grizzly did nothing wrong, either. When bears reach the sub-adult stage, they must leave their mothers and strike out on their own, foraging for a new area to live that is not already dominated by another adult bear. Sub-adults are often inexperienced, hungry, and on the move, and can be very dangerous to humans.

CHAPTER TWO

When Lewis and Clark First Met Grizzlies

Meriwether Lewis and William Clark

(Excerpted from the Journals of the Corps of Discovery.*)*

I ALWAYS FIND MYSELF READING THE JOURNALS OF LEWIS AND CLARK *with two mindsets. In one I am sharing and feeling the wonder of their second year (1805) on the high plains and mountains of the undiscovered American west. Every day they see teeming bison (buffalo) herds, elk, deer, antelope, beaver, birds, and waterfowl. Clark estimated one buffalo herd to number ten thousand. This idyllic life described in the* Journals *is interrupted by visions of the toil and hardships of the journey—the raging rivers, virtually impossible mountain passes, hailstorms and snow, and the demands of moving camps of men and supplies. The unedited versions of the* Journals *are difficult to read, with misspellings and gaps, but well worth the effort. In the excerpts we have here, we're focusing on the* Journal *pages that describe encounters with beasts larger and more ferocious than ever seen before: grizzly bears. At one point, Lewis wrote in his journal, "I would rather face 2 Indians than one grizzly bear." The Corps of Discovery had many "firsts" that would be recorded in American history. The text refers frequently to "brown" or "blonde" bears. These are grizzlies, as explained by Lewis in* Journal *entries to come.*

[Lewis, April 29, 1805]
Monday April 29th 1805.

Set out this morning at the usual hour; the wind was moderate; I walked on shore with one man. about 8 A.M. we fell in with two brown or yellow bear; both of which we wounded; one of them made his escape, the other after my firing on him pursued me seventy or eighty yards, but fortunately had been so badly wounded that he was unable to pursue so closely as to prevent my charging my gun; we again repeated our fir and killed him. it was a male not fully grown, we estimated his weight at 300 lbs. not having the means of ascertaining it precisely. The legs of this bear are somewhat longer than those of the black, as are it's tallons and tusks incomparably larger and longer. the testicles, which in the black bear are placed pretty well back between the thyes and contained in one pouch like those of the dog and most quadrupeds, are in the yellow or brown bear placed much further forward, and are suspended in seperate pouches from two to four inches asunder; it's colour is yellowish brown, the eyes small, black, and piercing; the front of the fore legs near the feet is usually black; the fur is finer thicker and deeper than that of the black bear. these are all the particulars in which this anamal appeared to me to differ from the black bear; it is a much more furious and formidable anamal, and will frequently pursue the hunter when wounded. it is asstonishing to see the wounds they will bear before they can be put to death. the Indians may well fear this anamal equiped as they generally are with their bows and arrows or indifferent fuzees, but in the hands of skillfull riflemen they are by no means as formidable or dangerous as they have been represented. game is still very abundant we can scarcely cast our eyes in any direction without percieving deer Elk Buffaloe or Antelopes. The quantity of wolves appear to increase in the same proportion; they generally hunt in parties of six eight or ten; they kill a great number of the Antelopes at this season; the Antelopes are yet meagre and the females are big with young; the wolves take them most generally in attempting to swim the river; in this manner my dog caught one drowned it and brought it on shore; they are but clumsey swimers, tho on land when in good order, they are extreemly fleet and dureable. we have frequently seen the wolves in pursuit of the Antelope in the plains; they appear to decoy a single one from a flock, and then pursue it, alturnately relieving each other untill they take it. on joining Capt Clark he informed me that he had seen a female and faun of the bighorned anamal; that they ran for some distance with great aparent ease along the side of the river bluff where it was almost perpendicular; two of the party fired on them while in motion without effect. we took the flesh of the bear on board and proceeded. Capt. Clark walked on shore this evening, killed a deer, and saw several of the bighorned anamals. there is more appearance of coal today than we have yet seen, the stratas are 6 feet thick in some instances; the earth has been birnt in many places, and always appears in stratas on the same level with the stratas of coal. we came too this evening in the mouth of a little river, which falls in on the Stard. side. This stream is about 50 yards wide from bank to bank; the water occupyes about 15 yards. the banks are of earth only, abrupt, tho not high—the bed, is of mud principally. Capt Clark, who was up this streeam about three miles, informed me that it continued about the same width, that it's current was gentle and it appeared navigable for perogus it meanders through an extensive, fertile, and beautifull vally as far as could bee seen about N. 30°W. there was but one solitary tree to be seen on the banks of this river after it left the bottom of the Missouri. the water of this river is clear, with a brownish yelow tint. here the highlands receede from the Missouri, leaving the vally formed by the river from seven to eight miles wide, and reather lower then usual.—This stream my friend Capt. C. named Marthas river

[Clark, April 29, 1805]
29th of April Monday 1805

Set out this morning at the usial hour. the wind is moderate &
from the N E had not proceeded far eer we Saw a female & her
faun of the Bighorn animal on the top of a Bluff lying, the noise we
made allarmed them and they came down on the Side of the bluff
which had but little Slope being nearly purpindicular, I directed
two men to kill those anamals, one went on the top and the other
man near the water they had two Shots at the doe while in motion
without effect, Those animals run & Skiped about with great ease
on this declivity & appeared to prefur it to the leavel bottom or
plain. Capt Lewis & one man walkd on Shore and he killed a
yellow Bear & the man with him wounded one other, after getting
the flesh of the bear on bord which was not far from the place we
brackfast, we proceeded on Saw 4 gangus of buffalow and great
numbers of Antelopes in every direction also Saw Elk and Several
wolves, I walked on Shore in the evening & killed a Deer which
was So meager as to be unfit for use The hills Contain more Coal,
and has a greater appearance of being burnt that below, the burnt
parts appear on a parrilel with the Stratiums of Coal, we Came
too in the mouth of a Little river on the S. S. which is about 50 or
60 yards from bank to bank, I was up this Stream 3 miles it continues its width and glides with a gentle Current, its water is about
15 yards wide at this time, and appears to be navagable for Canoes
&c. it meanders through a butifull & extencive vallie as far as can
be Seen about N 30° W. I saw only a Single tree in this fertile vallie
The water of the River is clear of a yellowish Colour, we call this
river Martheys river in honor to the Selebrated M. F Here the high

land widen from five to Eight miles and much lower than below, Saw Several of the big horn animals this evening. The Wolves distroy great numbers of the antilopes by decoying those animals Singularly out in the plains and prosueing them alternetly, those antelopes are Curious and will approach any thing which appears in motion near them &c.

[Lewis, May 5, 1805]
Sunday May 5th 1805

A fine they frequently also ascociate with the large geese when in flocks, but never saw them pared off with the large or common goose. The white brant ascociate in very large flocks, they do not appear to be mated or pared off as if they intended to raise their young in this quarter, I therefore doubt whether they reside here during the summer for that purpose.

this bird is about the size of the common brown brant or two thirds of the common goose, it is not so long by six inches from point to point of the wings when extended as the other; the beak head and neck are also larger and stronger; their beak legs and feet are of a redish or fleshcoloured white. the eye is of moderate size, the puple of a deep sea green incircled with a ring of yellowish brown. it has sixteen feathers of equal length in the tale; their note differs but little from the common brant, their flesh much the same, and in my opinion preferable to the goose, the flesh is dark. they are entirely of a beatifull pure white except the large feathers of the 1st and second joints of the wings which are jut black. form and habits are the same with the other brant; they sometimes ascociate and form one common flock. Capt Clark found a den of young wolves in the course of his walk today and also saw a great number of those anamals; they are very abundant in this quarter, and are of two species the small woolf or burrowing dog of the praries are the inhabitants almost invariably of the open plains; they usually ascociate in bands of ten or twelve sometimes more and burrow near some pass or place much frequented by game; not being able alone to take a deer or goat they are rarely ever found alone but hunt in bands; they frequently watch and seize their prey near their burrows; in these burrows they raise their young and to them they also resort when pursued; when a person approaches them they frequently bark, their note being precisely that of the small dog. they are of an intermediate size between that of the fox and dog, very active fleet and delicately formed; the ears large erect and pointed the head long and pointed more like that of the fox; tale long; the hair and fur also resembles the fox tho is much coarser and inferior. they are of a pale redish brown colour. the eye of a deep sea green colour small and piercing. their tallons are reather longer than those of the ordinary wolf or that common to the atlantic states, none of which are to be found in this quarter, nor I believe above the river Plat.—The large woolf found here is not as large as those of the atlantic states. they are lower and thicker made shorter leged. their colour which is not effected by the seasons, is a grey or blackish brown and every intermediate shade from that to a creen coloured white; these wolves resort the woodlands and are also found in the plains, but never take refuge in the ground or burrow so far as I have been able to inform myself. we scarcely see a gang of buffaloe without observing a parsel of those faithfull shepherds on their skirts in readiness to take care of the mamed & wounded. the large wolf never barks, but howls as those of the atlantic states do. Capt. Clark and Drewyer killed the largest brown bear this evening which we have yet seen. it was a most tremendious looking anamal, and extreemly hard to kill notwithstanding he had five balls through his lungs and five others in various parts he swam more than half the distance acoss the river to a sandbar & it was at least twenty minutes before he died; he did not attempt to attact, but fled and made the most tremendous roaring from the moment he was shot. We had no means of weighing this monster; Capt. Clark thought he would weigh 500 lbs. for my own part I think the estimate too small by 100 lbs. he measured 8 Feet 7½ Inches from the nose to the extremety of the hind feet, 5 F. to ½ Inch around the breast, 1 F. 11 I. arround the middle of the arm, & 3 F. 11 I. arround the neck; his tallons which were five in number on each foot were 4⅛ Inches in length. he was in good order, we therefore divided him among the party and made them boil the oil and put it in a cask for future uce; the oil is as hard as hogs lard when cool, much more so than that of the black bear. this bear differs from the common black bear in several respects; it's tallons are much longer and more blont, it's tale shorter, it's hair which is of a redish or bey brown, is longer thicker and finer than that of the black bear; his liver lungs and heart are much larger even in proportion with his size; the heart particularly was as large as that of a large Ox. his maw was also ten times the size of black bear, and was filled with flesh and fish. his testicles were pendant from the belly and placed four inches assunder in seperate bags or pouches.—this animal also feeds on roots and almost every species of wild fruit.

The party killed two Elk and a Buffaloe today, and my dog caught a goat, which he overtook by superior fleetness, the goat it must be understood was with young and extreemly poor. a great number of these goats are devowered by the wolves and bear at this season when they are poor and passing the river from S. W. to N. E. they are very inactive and easily taken in the water, a man can out swim them with great ease; the Indians take them in great numbers in the river at this season and in autumn when they repass to the S. W.

[Clark, May 5, 1805]
5th of May Sunday 1805

We Set out verry early and had not proceeded far before the rudder Irons of one of the Perogus broke which detained us a Short time Capt Lewis walked on Shore this morning and killed a Deer, after brackfast I walked on Shore Saw great numbers of Buffalow & Elk Saw also a Den of young wolves, and a number of grown wolves in every direction, the white & Grey Brant is in this part of the Missouri I shot at the white brant but at So great a distance I did not kill, The Countrey on both sides is as yesterday, handsom & fertile—The river rising & Current Strong & in the evening we Saw a Brown or Grisley beare on a Sand beech, I went out with one man Geo. Drewyer & Killed the bear, which was verry large and a turrible looking animal, which we found verry hard to kill we Shot ten Balls into him before we killed him, & 5 of those Balls through his lights This animal is the largest of the Carnivorous kind I ever Saw we had nothing that could way him, I think his weight may be Stated at 500 pounds, he measured 8 feet 7½ In. from his nose to the extremity of the Toe, 5 feet 10½ in. arround the breast, 1 feet 11 Ins. around the middle of the arm, 3 feet 11 Ins. arround the neck his tallents was 4 Inches & ⅜ long, he was good order, and appeared verry different from the Common black bear in as much as his tallents were blunt, his tail Short, his liver & lights much larger, his maw ten times as large and Contained meat or flesh & fish only—we had him Skined and divided, the oile tried up & put in Kegs for use. we Camped on the Stard Side, our men killed three Elk and a Buffalow to day, and our Dog Cought an antilope a fair race, this animal appeared verry pore & with young.

[Lewis, May 6, 1805]
Monday May 6th 1805.

The morning being fair and pleasant and wind favourable we set sale at an early hour, and proceeded on very well the greater part of the day; the country still continues level fertile and beautifull, the bottoms wide and well timbered comparitively speaking with other parts of the river; no appearance of birnt hills pumice stone or coal, the salts of tartar or vegitable salts continues to appear on the river banks, sand bars and in many parts of the plains most generally in the little revines at the base of the low hills. passed three streames today which discharged themselves on the Lard. side; the first of these we call little dry creek it contained some water in stand-ing pools but discharged none, the 2ed 50 yards wide no Water, we called it Big dry Creek, the 3rd is bed of a conspicuous river 200 yards wide which we called little dry river; the banks of these streams are low and bottoms wide with but little timber, their beds are almost entirely formed of a fine brown sand intermixed with a small proportion of little pebbles, which were either transparent, white, green, red, yellow or brown. these streams appeared to con-tinue their width without diminution as far as we could perceive them, which with rispect to the river was many miles, they had recenly discharged their waters. from the appearance of these streams, and the country through which they passed, we concluded that they had their souces in level low dry plains, which probably is the character of the country for a great distance west of this, or to the vicinity of the black hills, that the country being low on the same level nearly and in the same parallel of latitude, that the rains in the spring of the year suddonly melts the snow at the same time and causes for a few days a vast quantity of water which finds it's way to the Missouri through those channels; by reference to the diary of the weather &c it will be percieved that there is scarcely any rain during the summer Autumn and winter in this open country distant from the mountains. Fields still continues unwell. saw a brown bear swim the river above us, he disappeared before we can get in reach of him; I find that the curiossity of our party is pretty well satisfyed with rispect to this anamal, the formidable appearance of the male bear killed on the 5th added to the difficulty with which they die when even shot through the vital parts, has staggered the resolution several of them, others however seem keen for action with the bear; I expect these gentlemen will give us some amusement shotly as they soon begin now to coppolate. saw a great quantity of game of every species common here. Capt Clark walked on shore and killed two Elk, they were not in very good order, we therefore took a part of the meat only; it is now only amusement for Capt. C. and myself to kill as much meat as the party can consum; I hope it may continue thus through our whole rout, but this I do not much expect. two beaver were taken in traps this morning and one since shot by one of the party. saw numbers of these anamals peeping at us as we passed out of their wholes which they form of a cilindric shape, by burrowing in the face of the abbrupt banks of the river.

[Lewis, May 11, 1805]

About 5 P.M. my attention was struck by one of the Party runing at a distance towards us and making signs and hollowing as if in distress, I ordered the perogues to put too, and waited untill he arrived; I now found that it was Bratton the man with the soar hand whom I had permitted to walk on shore, he arrived so much out of breath that it was several minutes before he could tell what had happened; at length he informed me that in the woody bottom on the Lard. side about 1½ below us he had shot a brown bear which immediately turned on him and pursued him a considerable distance but he had wounded it so badly that it could not overtake him; I immediately turned out with seven of the party in quest of this monster, we at length found his trale and persued him about a mile by the blood through very thick brush of rosbushes and the large leafed willow; we finally found him concealed in some very thick brush and shot him through the skull with two balls; we proceeded dress him as soon as possible, we found him in good order; it was a monstrous beast, not quite so large as that we killed a few days past but in all other rispects much the same the hair is remarkably long fine and rich tho he appears parshally to have discharged his winter coat; we now found that Bratton had shot him through the center of the lungs, notwithstanding which he had pursued him near half a mile and had returned more than double that distance and with his tallons had prepared himself a bed in the earth of about 2 feet deep and five long and was perfectly alive when we found him which could not have been less than 2 hours after he received the wound; these bear being so hard to die reather intimedates us all; I must confess that I do not like the gentlemen and had reather fight two Indians than one bear; there is no other chance to conquer them by a single shot but by shooting them through the brains, and this becomes difficult in consequence of two large muscles which cover the sides of the forehead and the sharp projection of the center of the frontal bone, which is also of a pretty good thickness. the flece and skin were as much as two men could possibly carry. by the time we returned the sun had set and I determined to remain here all night, and directed the cooks to render the bear's oil and put it in the kegs which was done. there was about eight gallons of it.

[Clark, May 11, 1805]
May the 11th Satturday 1805.

Wind hard fore part of last night the latter part verry Cold a white frost this morning, the river riseing a little and verry Crooked the high land is rugged and approaches nearer than below, the hills and bluff exhibit more mineral quats & Salts than below, the gullies in maney places are white, and their bottoms one, two & 3 Inches deep of this mineral, no appearance of either burnt pumice Stone or Coal, the Countrey hilley on both Sides of a rich black earth, which disolves This kind of Countrey Continues of the Same quallity for maney miles on either Side, we observed Some hills which appeared to be timbered, I walked to this timber and found it to pitch pine & Dwarf Cedar, we observe in every derection Buffalow, Elk, Antelopes & Mule deer inumerable and So jintle that we Could approach near them with great ease, I killed 2 Mule Deer for the benifit of their Skins for the party, and about the place I expected the party would get to Camp I killed 2 fat Bulls for theire use, in my absence they had killed a fine fat Yellow bear below which detained them and they did not reach the place I expected, but had Camped on the Lard. Side about 2 miles below on my return to the party I killed a fat Beaver the wind blew verry hard from the S. W. all the after part of this day which retarded our progress verry much. river rose 2 In

[Clark, May 13, 1805]
13th of May Monday 1805

The wind Continued to blow hard untill one oClock P M. today at which time it fell a little and we Set out and proceeded on verry well about 9 miles and Camped on the Lard Side. the countrey much the Same appearance as yesterday but little timber in the bottoms; Some Pine in places on the Stard. Hills. I killed two deer this evening one a mule deer & the other a common Deer, the party killed Several this morning all for the use of their Skins which are now good, one man Gibson wounded a verry large brown bear, too late this evening to prosue him—We passed two Creeks in a bend to the Lard Side neither them had any water, are somewhat wider; passed some high black bluffs. saw immence herds of buf-faloe today also Elk deer wolves and Antelopes. passed three large creeks one on the Stard. and two others on the Lard. side, neither of which had any runing water. Capt Clark walked on shore and killed a very fine buffaloe cow. I felt an inclination to eat some veal and walked on shore and killed a very fine buffaloe calf and a large woolf, much the whitest I had seen, it was quite as white as the wool of the common sheep. one of the party wounded a brown bear very badly, but being alone did not think proper to pursue him. In the evening the men in two of the rear canoes discovered a large brown bear lying in the open grounds about 300 paces from the river, and six of them went out to attack him, all good hunters; they took the advantage of a small eminence which concealed them and got within 40 paces of him unperceived, two of them reserved their fires as had been previously conscerted, the four others fired nearly at the same time and put each his bullet through him, two of the balls passed through the bulk of both lobes of his lungs, in an instant this monster ran at them with open mouth, the two who had reserved their fires discharged their pieces at him as he came towards them, boath of them struck him, one only slightly and the other fortunately broke his shoulder, this however only retarded his motion for a moment only, the men unable to reload their guns took to flight, the bear pursued and had very nearly overtaken them before they reached the river; two of the party betook themselves to a canoe and the others seperated an concealed themselves among the willows, reloaded their pieces, each discharged his piece at him as they had an opportunity they struck him several times again but the guns served only to direct the bear to them, in this manner he pursued two of them seperately so close that they were obliged to throw aside their guns and pouches and throw themselves into the river altho the bank was nearly twenty feet perpendicular; so enraged was this anamal that he plunged into the river only a few feet behind the second man he had compelled take refuge in the water, when one of those who still remained on shore shot him through the head and finally killed him; they then took him on shore and butched him when they found eight balls had passed through him in different directions; the bear being old the flesh was indifferent, they therefore only took the skin and fleece, the latter made us several gallons of oil; it was after the sun had set before these men come up with us, where we had been halted by an occurrence, which I have now to recappitulate, and which altho happily passed without ruinous injury, I cannot recollect but with the utmost trepidation and horror; this is the upseting and narrow escape of the white perogue It happened unfortunately for us this evening that Charbono was at the helm of this Perogue, in stead of Drewyer, who had previously steered her; Charbono cannot swim and is perhaps the most timid waterman in the world; perhaps it was equally unluckey that Capt. C. and myself were both on shore at that moment, a circumstance which rarely happened; and tho we were on the shore opposite to the perogue, were too far distant to be heard or to do more than remain spectators of her fate; in this perogue _____ were embarked, our papers, Instruments, books medicine, a great part of our merchandize and in short almost every article indispensibly necessary to further the views, or insure the success of the enterprize in which we are now launched to the distance of 2200 miles. surfice it to say, that the Perogue was under sail when a sudon squawl of wind struck her obliquely, and turned her considerably, the steersman allarmed, in stead of puting her before the wind, lufted her up into it, the wind was so violent that it drew the brace of the squarsail out of the hand of the man who was attending it, and instantly upset the perogue and would have turned her completely topsaturva, had it not have been from the resistance mad by the oarning against the water; in this situation Capt. C and myself both fired our guns to attract the attention if possible of the crew and ordered the halyards to be cut and the sail hawled in, but they did not hear us; such was their confusion and consternation at this moment, that they suffered the perogue to lye on her side for half a minute before they took the sail in, the perogue then wrighted but had filled within an inch of the gunwals; Charbono still crying to his god for mercy, had not yet recollected the rudder, nor could the repeated orders of the Bowsman, Cruzat, bring him to his recollection untill he threatend to shoot him instantly if he did not take hold of the rudder and do his duty, the waves by this time were runing very high, but the fortitude resolution and good conduct of Cruzat saved her; he ordered 2 of the men to throw out the water with some kettles that fortunately were convenient, while himself and two others rowed her ashore, where she arrived scarcely above the water; we now took every article out of her and lay them to drane as well as we could for the evening, baled out the canoe and secured her; there were two other men beside Charbono on board who could not swim, and who of course must also have perished had the perogue gone to the bottom. while the perogue lay on her side, finding I could not be heard, I for a moment forgot my own situation, and involluntarily droped my gun, threw aside my shot pouch and was in the act of unbuttoning my coat, before I recollected the folly of the attempt I was about to make, which was to throw myself into the river and indevour to swim to the perogue; the perogue was three hundred yards distant the waves so high that a perogue could scarcely live in any situation, the water excessively could, and the stream rappid; had I undertaken this project therefore, there was a hundred to one but what I should have paid the forfit of my life for the madness of my project, but this had the perogue been lost, I should have valued but little.—After having all matters arranged for the evening as well as the nature of circumstances would permit, we thought it a proper occasion to console ourselves and cheer the sperits of our men and accordingly took a drink of grog and gave each man a gill of sperits.

[Lewis, May 19, 1805]
Sunday May 19th 1805.

The last night was disagreeably could; we were unable to set out untill 8 oclock A.M. in consequence of a heavy fogg, which obscured the river in such a manner that we could not see our way; this is the first we have experienced in any thing like so great a degree; there was also a fall of due last evening, which is the second we have experienced since we have entered this extensive open country. at eight we set out and proceeded as yesterday by means of the cord principally, the hills are high and the country similar to that of yesterday. Capt Clark walked on shore with two of the hunters and killed a brown bear; notwithstanding that it was shot through the heart it ran at it's usual pace near a quarter of a mile before it fell. one of the party wounded a beaver, and my dog as usual swam in to catch it; the beaver bit him through the hind leg and cut the artery; it was with great difficulty that I could stop the blood; I fear it will yet prove fatal to him. on Capt. Clark's return he informed me that he had from the top of one of the adjacent hights discovered the entrance of a large stream which discharged itself into the Missouri on the Lard. side distant 6 or seven miles; from the same place he also saw a range of Mountains, bearing W. distant 40 or 50 miles; they appeared to proceed in a S. S. W. direction; the N. N. E. extremity of these mountains appeared abrupt. This afternoon the river was croked, rappid and containing more sawyers than we have seen in the same space since we left the entrance of the river Platte. Capt. C. in the course of his walk killed three deer and a beaver, I also walked on shore this evening a few miles and killed an Elk, a buck, and a beaver. the party killed and caught 4 other beaver & 3 deer.

The men complain much of sore eyes and imposthumes.

[Clark, May 19, 1805]
May 19th Sunday 1805

a verry cold night, the murckery Stood at 38 at 8 oClock this morning, a heavy dew which is the 2d I have Seen this Spring. The fog (which was the first) was So thick this morning that we could not Set out untill the Sun was about 2 hours up, at which time a Small breeze Sprung up from the E. which Cleared off the fog & we proceeded on by means of the Cord The hills are high & rugged the Countrey as yesterday—I walked on Shore with two men we killed a white or grey bear; not withstanding that it was Shot through the heart it ran at it's usial pace near a quarter of a mile before it fell. Capt Lewis's dog was badly bitten by a wounded beaver and was near bleading to death—. after killing the Bear I continued my walk alone, & killed 3 Deer & a Beaver; finding that the Perogues were below I assended the highest hill I could See, from the top of which I Saw the mouth of M. Shell R & the meanderings of the Missouri for a long distance. I also Saw a high mountain in a westerley direction, bearing S. S W. about 40 or 50 miles distant, in the evening the river was verry Crooked and much more rapid & Containing more Sawyers than any which we have passed above the River Platte Capt Lewis walked on Shore this after noon & killed an Elk, Buck & a Beaver, I kiled three Deer at dinner, the hunters killed three other Deer to day Several beaver also killed. We Camped on the Stard Side in a bottom of Small Cotton wood

[Lewis, May 22, 1805]
Wednesday May 22cd 1805.

I killed a deer in the course of my walk today. Capt. C. also walked out this evening and took a view of the country from a conspicuous point and found it the same as has been discribed. we have caught but few fish since we left the Mandans, they do not bite freely, what we took were the white cat of 2 to 5 lbs. I presume that fish are scarce in this part of the river. We encamped earlyer this evening than usual in order render the oil of a bear which we killed. I do not believe that the Black bear common to the lower part of this river and the Atlantic States, exists in this quarter; we have neither seen one of them nor their tracks which would be easily distinguished by it's shortness of tallons when compared with the brown grizly or white bear. I believe that it is the same species or family of bears which assumes all those colours at different ages and seasons of the year.

[Lewis, June 13, 1805]
Thursday June 13th 1805.

I am induced to believe that the Brown, the white and the Grizly bear of this country are the same species only differing in colour from age or more probably from the same natural cause that many other anamals of the same family differ in colour. one of those which we killed yesterday was of a creemcoloured white while the other in company with it was of the common bey or rdish brown, which seems to be the most usual colour of them. the white one appeared from it's tallons and teath to be the youngest; it was smaller than the other, and although a monstrous beast we supposed that it had not yet attained it's growth and that it was a little upwards of two years old. the young cubs which we have killed have always been of a brownish white, but none of them as white as that we killed yesterday. one other that we killed sometime since which I mentioned sunk under some driftwood and was lost, had a white stripe or list of about eleven inches wide entirely arround his body just behind the shoalders, and was much darker than these bear usually are. the grizly bear we have never yet seen. I have seen their tallons in possession of the Indians and from their form I am perswaded if there is any difference between this species and the brown or white bear it is very inconsiderable. There is no such anamal as a black bear in this open country or of that species generally denominated the black bear

my fare is really sumptuous this evening; buffaloe's humps, tongues and marrowbones, fine trout parched meal pepper and salt, and a good appetite; the last is not considered the least of the luxuries.

[Clark, June 11, 1805]
June 11th Tuesday 1805

a fair morning wind from the S W. hard we burry 1 keg in the Cash & 2 Canisters of Powder in 2 seperate places all with Lead; & in the Cash 2 axes, auger, Plains, 1 Keg flour, 2 Kegs Pork, 2 Kegs Parchd meal 1 Keg salt, files Chisel, 2 Musquits, Some tin cups, bowel, 3 bear Skins, Beaver Skins, Horns, & parts of the mens robes & clothes.—Beaver Traps and blacksmith's tools. Capt. Lewis Set out at 8 oClock we delayed to repare Some guns out of order & complete our deposit, which took us the day the evening fair and fine wind from the N. W. after night it became cold & the wind blew hard, the Indian woman verry Sick, I blead her which appeared to be of great Service to her both rivers riseing fast

[Lewis, June 12, 1805]
Wednesday June 12th 1805.

This morning I felt myself quite revived, took another portion of my decoction and set out at sunrise. I now boar out from the river in order to avoid the steep ravines of the river which usually make out in the plain to the distance of one or two miles; after gaining the leavel plain my couse was a litte to the West of S. W.—having traveled about 12 miles by 9 in the morning, the sun became warm, and I boar a little to the south in order to gain the river as well to obtain water to allay my thirst as to kill something for breakfast; for the plain through which we had been passing possesses no water and is so level that we cannot approach the buffaloe within shot before they discover us and take to flight. we arrived at the river about 10 A.M. having traveled about 15 m. at this place there is a handsom open bottom with some cottonwood timber, here we met with two large bear, and killed them boath at the first fire, a circumstance which I beleive has never happend with the party in killing the brown bear before. we dressed the bear, breakfasted on a part of one of them and hung the meat and skins on the trees out of the reach of the wolves. I left a note on a stick near the river for Capt. Clark, informing him of my progress &c.—after refreshing ourselves abut 2 hours we again ascended the bluffs and gained the high plain; saw a great number of burrowing squirrels in the plains today. also wolves Antelopes mule deer and immence herds of buffaloe. we passed a ridge of land considerably higher than the adjacent plain on either side, from this hight we had a most beatifull and picturesk view of the Rocky mountains which wer perfectly covered with Snow and reaching from S. E. to the N. of N. W.—they appear to be formed of several ranges each succeeding range rising higher than the preceding one untill the most distant appear to loose their snowey tops in the clouds; this was an august spectacle and still rendered more formidable by the recollection that we had them to pass. we traveled about twelve miles when we agin struck the Missoury at a handsome little bottom of Cottonwood timber and altho the sun had not yet set I felt myself somewhat weary being weakened I presume by late disorder; and therfore determined to remain here during the ballance of the day and night, having marched about 27 miles today. on our way in the evening we had killed a buffaloe, an Antelope and three mule deer, and taken a sufficient quantity of the best of the flesh of these anamals for three meals, which we had brought with us. This evening I ate very heartily and after pening the transactions of the day amused myself catching those white fish mentioned yesterday; they are here in great abundance I caught upwards of a douzen in a few minutes; they bit most freely at the melt of a deer which goodrich had brought with him for the purpose of fishing.

The narrow leafed cottonwood grows here in common with the other species of the same tree with a broad leaf or that which has constituted the major part of the timber of the Missouri from it's junction with the Mississippi to this place. The narrow leafed cottonwood differs only from the other in the shape of it's leaf and greater thickness of it's bark. the leaf is a long oval acutely pointed, about 2½ or 3 Inches long and from ¾ to an inch in width; it is thick, sometimes slightly grooved or channeled; margin slightly serrate; the upper disk of a common green while the under disk is of a whiteish green; the leaf is smoth. the beaver appear to be extremely fond of this tree and even seem to scelect it from among the other species of Cottonwood, probably from it's affording a deeper and softer bark than the other species.—saw some sign of the Otter as well as beaver near our camp, also a great number of tracks of the brown bear; these fellows leave a formidable impression in the mud or sand I measured one this evening which was eleven inches long exclusive of the tallons and seven and ¼ in width.

[Clark, June 12, 1805]
June 12th 1805 Wednesday

last night was Clear and Cold, this morning fair we Set out at 8 oClock & proceeded on verry well wind from the S. W. The interpreters wife verry Sick So much So that I move her into the back part of our Covered part of the Perogue which is Cool, her own situation being a verry hot one in the bottom of the Perogue exposed to the Sun—Saw emence No. of Swallows in the 1st bluff on the Lard. Side, water verry Swift, the bluff are blackish Clay & Coal for about 80 feet. the earth above that for 30 or 40 feet is a brownish yellow, a number of bars of corse gravil and Stones of different Shape & Size &c. Saw a number of rattle Snakes to day one of the men cought one by the head in Catch'g hold of a bush on which his head lay reclined three canoes were in great danger today one diped water, another was near turning over &c. at 2 oClock P M a fiew drops of rain I walked thro a point and killed a Buck Elk & Deer, and we camped on the Stard Side, the Interpreters woman verry Sick worse than She has been. I give her medison one man have a fellon riseing on his hand one other with the Tooth ake has taken cold in the jaw &c.

[Lewis, June 13, 1805]
Thursday June 13th 1805.

I am induced to believe that the Brown, the white and the Grizly bear of this country are the same species only differing in colour from age or more probably from the same natural cause that many other anamals of the same family differ in colour. one of those which we killed yesterday was of a creemcoloured white while the other in company with it was of the common bey or rdish brown, which seems to be the most usual colour of them. the white one appeared from it's tallons and teath to be the youngest; it was smaller than the other, and although a monstrous beast we supposed that it had not yet attained it's growth and that it was a little upwards of two years old. the young cubs which we have killed have always been of a brownish white, but none of them as white as that we killed yesterday. one other that we killed sometime since which I mentioned sunk under some driftwood and was lost, had a white stripe or list of about eleven inches wide entirely arround his body just behind the shoalders, and was much darker than these bear usually are. the grizly bear we have never yet seen. I have seen their tallons in possession of the Indians and from their form I am perswaded if there is any difference between this species and the brown or white bear it is very inconsiderable. There is no such anamal as a black bear in this open country or of that species generally denominated the black bear

my fare is really sumptuous this evening; buffaloe's humps, tongues and marrowbones, fine trout parched meal pepper and salt, and a good appetite; the last is not considered the least of the luxuries.

WOLVES
[Lewis, June 14, 1805]
Friday June 14th 1805.

This morning at sunrise I dispatched Joseph Fields with a letter to Capt. Clark and ordered him to keep sufficiently near the river to observe it's situation in order that he might be enabled to give Capt. Clark an idea of the point at which it would be best to halt to make our portage. I set one man about preparing a saffold and collecting wood to dry the meat Sent the others to bring in the ballance of the buffaloe meat, or at least the part which the wolves had left us, for those fellows are ever at hand and ready to partake with us the moment we kill a buffaloe; and there is no means of puting the meat out of their reach in those plains; the two men shortly after returned with the meat and informed me that the wolves had devoured the greater part of the meat. about ten OClock this morning while the men were engaged with the meat I took my Gun and espontoon and thought I would walk a few miles and see where the rappids termineated above, and return to dinner. accordingly I set out and proceeded up the river about S. W. after passing one continued in these plains and more particularly in the valley just below me immence herds of buffaloe are feeding. the missouri just above this hill makes a bend to the South where it lies a smoth even and unruffled sheet of water of nearly a mile in width bearing on it's watry bosome vast flocks of geese which feed at pleasure in the delightfull pasture on either border. the young geese are now completely feathered except the wings which both in the young and old are yet deficient. after feasting my eyes on this ravishing prospect and resting myself a few minutes I determined to procede as far as the river which I saw discharge itself on the West side of the Missouri convinced that it was the river which the Indians call medicine river and which they informed us fell into the Missouri just above the falls I decended the hills and directed my course to the bend of the Missouri near which there was a herd of at least a thousand buffaloe; here I thought it would be well to kill a buffaloe and leave him untill my return from the river and if I then found that I had not time to get back to camp this evening to remain all night here there being a few sticks of drift wood lying along shore which would answer for my fire, and a few sattering cottonwood trees a few hundred yards below which would afford me at least a semblance of a shelter. under this impression I scelected a fat buffaloe and shot him very well, through the lungs; while I was gazeing attentively on the poor anamal discharging blood in streams from his mouth and nostrils, expecting him to fall every instant, and having entirely forgotton to reload my rifle, a large white, or reather brown bear, had perceived and crept on me within 20 steps before I discovered him; in the first moment I drew up my gun to shoot, but at the same instant recolected that she was not loaded and that he was too near for me to hope to perform this opperation before he reached me, as he was then briskly advancing on me; it was an open level plain, not a bush within miles nor a tree within less than three hundred yards of me; the river bank was sloping and not more than three feet above the level of the water; in short there was no place by means of which I could conceal myself from this monster untill I could charge my rifle; in this situation I thought of retreating in a brisk walk as fast as he was advancing untill I could reach a tree about 300 yards below me, but I had no sooner terned myself about but he pitched at me, open mouthed and full speed, I ran about 80 yards and found he gained on me fast, I then run into the water the idea struk me to get into the water to such debth that I could stand and he would be obliged to swim, and that I could in that situation defend myself with my espontoon; accordingly I ran haistily into the water about waist deep, and faced about and presented the point of my espontoon, at this instant he arrived at the edge of the water within about 20 feet of me; the moment I put myself in this attitude of defence he sudonly wheeled about as if frightened, declined the combat on such unequal grounds, and retreated with quite as great precipitation as he had just before pursued me. as soon as I saw him run off in that manner I returned to the shore and charged my gun, which I had still retained in my hand throughout this curious adventure. I saw him run through the level open plain about three miles, till he disappeared in the woods on medecine river; during the whole of this distance he ran at full speed, sometimes appearing to look behind him as if he expected pursuit. I now began to reflect on this novil occurrence and indeavoured to account for this sudden retreat of the bear. I at first thought that perhaps he had not smelt me before he arrived at the waters edge so near me, but I then reflected that he had pursued me for about 80 or 90 yards before I took the water and on examination saw the grownd toarn with his tallons immediately on the impression of my steps; and the cause of his allarm still remains with me misterious and unaccountable.—so it was and I feelt myself not a little gratifyed that he had declined the combat. My gun reloaded I felt confidence once more in my strength; and determined not to be thwarted in my design of visiting medicine river, but determined never again to suffer my peice to be longer empty than the time she necessarily required to charge her. I passed through the plain nearly in the direction which the bear had run to medecine river, found it a handsome stream, about 200 yds. wide with a gentle current, apparently deep, it's waters clear, and banks which were formed principally of darkbrown and blue clay were about the hight of those of the Missouri or from 3 to 5 feet; yet they had not the appearance of ever being overflown, a circumstance, which I did not expect so immediately in the neighbourhood of the mountains, from whence I should have supposed, that sudden and immence torrants would issue at certain seasons of the year; but the reverse is absolutely the case. I am therefore compelled to beleive that the snowey mountains yeald their warters slowly, being partially effected every day by the influence of the sun only, and never suddonly melted down by haisty showers of rain.

having examined Medecine river I now determined to return, having by my estimate about 12 miles to walk. I looked at my watch and found it was half after six P.M.—in returning through the level bottom of Medecine river and about 200 yards distant from the Missouri, my direction led me directly to an anamal that I at first supposed was a wolf; but on nearer approach or about sixty paces distant I discovered that it was not, it's colour was a brownish yellow; it was standing near it's burrow, and when I approached it thus nearly, it couched itself down like a cat looking immediately at me as if it designed to spring on me. I took aim at it and fired, it instantly disappeared in it's burrow; I loaded my gun and exmined the place which was dusty and saw the track from which I am still further convinced that it was of the tiger kind. whether I struck it or not I could not determine, but I am almost confident that I did; my gun is true and I had a steady rest by means of my espontoon, which I have found very serviceable to me in this way in the open plains. It now seemed to me that all the beasts of the neighbourhood had made a league to distroy me, or that some fortune was disposed to amuse herself at my expence, for I had not proceded more than three hundred yards from the burrow of this tyger cat, before three bull buffaloe, which wer feeding with a large herd about half a mile from me on my left, seperated from the herd and ran full speed towards me, I thought at least to give them some amusement and altered my direction to meet them; when they arrived within a hundred yards they mad a halt, took a good view of me and retreated with precipitation. I then continued my rout homewards passed the buffaloe which I had killed, but did not think it prudent to remain all night at this place which really from the succession of curious adventures wore the impression on my mind of inchantment; at sometimes for a moment I thought it might be a dream, but the prickley pears which pierced my feet very severely once in a while, particularly after it grew dark, convinced me that I was really awake, and that it was necessary to make the best of my way to camp. it was sometime after dark before I returned to the party; I found them extremely uneasy for my safety; they had formed a thousand conjectures, all of which equally forboding my death, which they had so far settled among them, that they had already agreed on the rout which each should take in the morning to surch for me. I felt myself much fortiegued, but eat a hearty supper and took a good night's rest.—the weather being warm I had left my leather over shirt and had woarn only a yellow flannin one.

Soon after we Camped two ganges of Buffalow crossed one above & the other below we killed 7 of them & a calf and Saved as much of the best of the meat as we could this evening, one man A Willard going for a load of meat at 170 yards distance on an Island was attact by a white bear and verry near being Caught, prosued within 40 yards of Camp where I was with one man I collected 3 others of the party and prosued the bear (who had prosued my track from a buffalow I had killed on the Island at about 300 yards distance and chance to meet Willard) for fear of his attacking one man Colter at the lower point of the Island, before we had got down the bear had allarmed the man and prosued him into the water, at our approach he retreated, and we relieved the man in the water, I Saw the bear but the bushes was So thick that I could not Shoot him and it was nearly dark, the wind from the S W & Cool killed a beaver & an elk for their Skins this evening

[Lewis, June 25, 1805]
Tuesday June 25th 1805.

This morning early I sent the party back to the lower camp; dispatched Frazier down with the canoe for Drewyer and the meat he had collected, and Joseph Fields up the Missouri to hunt Elk. at eight OCIk. sent Gass and Sheilds over to the large Island for bark and timber. about noon Fields returned and informed me that he had seen two white bear near the river a few miles above and in attempting to get a shoot them had stumbled uppon a third which immediately made at him being only a few steps distant; that in runing in order to escape from the bear he had leaped down a steep bank of the river on a stony bar where he fell cut his hand bruised his knees and bent his gun. that fortunately for him the bank hid him from the bear when he fell and that by that means he had escaped. this man has been truly unfortunate with these bear, this is the second time that he has narrowly escaped from them.

[Clark, June 25, 1805]
June 25th Tuesday 1805

a fair worm morning, Clouded & a few drops of rain at 5 oClock A.M. fair I feel my Self a little unwell with a looseness &c. &c. put out the Stores to dry & Set Chabonah &c to Cook for the party against their return—he being the only man left on this Side with me I had a little Coffee for brackfast which was to me a riarity as I had not tasted any Since last winter.—it may be here worthy of remark that the Sales were hoised in the Canoes as the men were drawing them and the wind was great relief to them being

Sufficeritly Strong to move the Canoes on the Trucks, this is Sale-
ing on Dry land in every Sence of the word, Serjeant N Pryor Sick,
the party amused themselves with danceing untill 10 oClock all
Chearfullness and good humer, they all tied up their loads to make
an early Start in the morning.

[Lewis, June 27, 1805]
Thursday June 27th 1805.

The party returned early this morning for the remaining canoe and
baggage; Whitehouse was not quite well this morning I therefore
detained him and about 10 A.M. set him at work with Frazier
sewing the skins together for the boat; Shields and Gass continued
the operation of shaving and fiting the horizontall bars of wood in
the sections of the boat; the timber is so crooked and indifferent
that they make but little progress, for myself I continued to act the
part of cook in order to keep all hands employed. some Elk came
near our camp and we killed 2 of them at 1 P.M. a cloud arrose to
the S. W. and shortly after came on attended with violent Thunder
Lightning and hail &c. (see notes on diary of the weather for June).
soon after this storm was over Drewyer and J. Fields returned. they
were about 4 miles above us during the storm, the hail was of no
uncommon size where they were. They had killed 9 Elk and three
bear during their absence; one of the bear was the largest by far that
we have yet seen; the skin appear to me to be as large as a common
ox. while hunting they saw a thick brushey bottom on the bank
of the river where from the tracks along shore they suspected that
there were bare concealed; they therefore landed without making
any nois and climbed a leaning tree and placed themselves on it's

branches about 20 feet above the ground, when thus securely fixed they gave a hoop and this large bear instantly rushed forward to the place from whence he had heard the human voice issue, when he arrived at the tree he made a short paus and Drewyer shot him in the head. it is worthy of remark that these bear never climb. the fore feet of this bear measured nine inches across and the hind feet eleven and—3/4 in length & exclusive of the tallons and seven inches in width. a bear came within thirty yards of our camp last night and eat up about thirty weight of buffaloe suit which was hanging on a pole. my dog seems to be in a constant state of alarm with these bear and keeps barking all night. soon after the storm this evening the water on this side of the river became of a deep crimson colour which I pesume proceeded from some stream above and on this side. there is a kind of soft red stone in the bluffs and bottoms. of the gullies in this neighbourhood which forms this colouring matter.—At the lower camp. Capt. Clark completed a draught of the river with the couses and distances from the entrance of the Missouri to Ft. Mandan, which we intend depositing here in order to guard against accedents. Sergt. Pryor is somewhat better this morning. at 4 P.M. the party returned from the upper camp; Capt. C. gave them a drink of grog; they prepared for the labour of the next day. soon after the party returned it began to rain accompanyed by some hail and continued a short time; a second shower fell late in the evening accompanyed by a high wind from N. W.—the mangled carcases of several buffaloe pass down the river today which had no doubt perished in the falls.

[Lewis, July 2, 1805]
Tuesday July 2cd 1805

A shower of rain fell very early this morning after which we dispatched the men for the remaining baggage at the 6 mile stake.
Shields and Bratton seting their tarkiln, Sergts. Pryor and Gass at
work on the waystrips and myself and all other hands engaged in
puting the boat together which we accomplished in about 3 hours
and I then set four men at work sewing the leather over the cross
bars of Iron on the inner side of the boat, which form the ends of
the sections. about 2 P.M. the party returned with the baggage,
all well pleased that they had completed the laborious task of the
portage. The Musquetoes uncommonly troublesome the wind hard
from the S. W. all day I think it possible that these almost perpetual
S. W. winds proceede from the agency of the Snowey Mountains
and the wide level and untimbered plains which streach themselves
along their bases for an immence distance (i e) that the air comeing
in contact with the snow is suddonly chilled and condenced, thus
becoming heaver than the air beneath in the plains, it glides down
the sides of these mountains & decends to the plains, where by the
constant action of the sun on the face of an untimbered country
there is a partial vacuum formed for it's reception. I have observed
that the winds from this quarter are always the coldest and most
violent which we experience, yet I am far from giving full credit to
my own hypothesis on this subject; if hoever I find on the opposite
side of these mountains that the winds take a contrary direction I
shall then have more faith. After I had completed my observation
of Equal Altitudes today Capt. Clark Myself and 12 men passed
over to the large Island to hunt bear. the brush in that part of it

where the bear frequent is an almost impenetrable thicket of the broad leafed willow; this brush we entered in small parties of 3 or four together and surched in every part. we found one only which made at Drewyer and he shot him in the brest at the distance of about 20 feet, the ball fortunately passed through his heart, the stroke knocked the bear down and gave Drewyer time to get out of his sight; the bear changed his course we pursued him about a hundred yards by the blood and found him dead; we surched the thicket in every part but found no other, and therefore returned. this was a young male and would weigh about 400 lbs.

CHAPTER THREE

The Grizzly on the Elk Mountain Trail

Kathleen Snow

(Excerpted from Taken by Bear in Glacier National Park, *Lyons Press, 2020.)*

THE CHANCE TO PHOTOGRAPH A GRIZZLY WITH THREE CUBS IN THE GLA-
cier Park backcountry seemed heaven-sent to Chuck Gibbs. He clicked on
several images, as he got closer and closer—then, too close! Finally, a tree
that he climbed and a .45-caliber handgun couldn't save him.

National Park Service–Glacier Park
Case Incident Record Number 870092
Location: Southwestern Glacier Park, Elk Mountain
Date/Time: Saturday, April 25, 1987, approximately 6:00 p.m.
Remains found April 26, 1987

She was golden-tan and beautiful. Even more unusual, she had
raised three similarly tan young ones to near adulthood, despite the
perils of food finding and the marauding of males. This family of
four stayed close, exploring Glacier Park together.

Chuck Gibbs was a loving husband who carried his wife
(recovering from surgery) twice across the stream on that final day.
He was a photographer and a school bus driver, and he practiced
the art of photography for art's sake, and because he needed extra
money.

This Glacier Park grizzly mother and the man who loved to
be out in nature—whether hiking, hunting (he was an expert
marksman), or taking photographs—came together on April 25,
1987. That Saturday, the late-April Glacier Park sun shone upon
Charles "Chuck" Gibbs and his wife [name redacted] at the far
southwestern boundary of the Park, the temperature reaching the
high 50s. The couple started up the Fielding Trail near the Fielding Patrol Cabin at about 11:15 a.m. Their plan was to hike to Ole
Creek and then return. The sky was clear, with no precipitation.

Nature seemed benign. They parked their camper truck on the access road, leaving their civilized comforts behind.

Born in Virginia, Chuck was a six-foot-tall Montanan with short brown hair and a mustache. He carried his camera bag, including a 400 mm telephoto lens for close-ups.

At 2:00 p.m. Chuck and his wife arrived at Ole Creek, and at 3:00 p.m. left Ole Creek for the hike back to the trailhead. Their return hike was interrupted when Chuck spotted something on the southwest flank of Elk Mountain, high up beyond wooded brush. Chuck had an unusual ability to spot wildlife, either with the naked eye or through binoculars, even when the wildlife resembled nothing more than a dot. Movement of the dot caught his attention; even when at rest, his talent could spot the living creature.

"On Friday afternoon on entering the park," Chuck's wife said, "we stopped at the Goat Lick and he hiked quite a ways up the top of that mountain to photograph some goats that he spotted up there."

Excerpts from her interview with the ranger [name redacted] on May 14, 1987, appear below.

Most of the people just kind of looked at the bridge, you know, from a distance, that was fine, but he got right on up to the top of the hill—I did not go with him at that time. I've been recuperating from surgery about three weeks ago, and I was just resting in the truck. And he came down and he was pointing it out to some local tourists, where all the goats were, and also looked over to the left and no one would have seen those, but he saw a herd of elk, and let people look through his binoculars at the elk too.

They were kind of impressed that he could spot all those animals, you know. Real readily; [he] had a really keen eye in the woods.

[It was] a beautiful afternoon on Saturday. We ate an early lunch around 11 o'clock and headed up the trail. . . . I kept hiking along very, very slowly, just taking my time and just enjoying the day. It was beautiful and just good to be out again. . . . He was going very slowly with me. At that time we came to a larger creek. I'd stepped across two previous creeks before the ranger cabin and got to that and I thought that was going to be my turning-around point, because I thought I wasn't quite up to fording the stream. And he picked me up and carried me across.

We headed on back, and he stopped and was glassing over to the left at some avalanche chutes that he thought, you know, looked like [they] could be promising for grizzlies.

He thought with his naked eye that he had spotted a grizzly just from where we were looking back over to those clearings. It just looked like a dot, but you know, he's real uncanny about picking up things like that. I would have walked right back past the trail and never have [known] there was a grizzly within miles, and he spotted the grizzly, and first he saw two cubs, and then he handed me the binoculars and I saw them. . . . I said, Yeah, it's with three cubs. They were yearlings; they weren't this year's cubs, so they looked to be pretty good-size cubs.

I looked through the binoculars some more as he was watching them through the camera lens, and maybe taking a couple shots. And he commented to me at that point that the Lord had really been good to him, to share seeing so many grizzlies in Montana.

After we had sat there and watched the grizzlies and commented on how neat it was to spot them in the wilderness. . . . He was just kind of joking around [and] asked me what I would do, or said that if he was attacked, he would try to climb a tree, and said, What would you do?

I said I'm not a good tree climber—but I'd probably give it a good try, too, if I possibly could. . . . You know, he just seemed kind of content just to see them—it was the first spotting of the spring, and [he] got real excited by that, and the fact that there were three cubs, which we had never seen before. . . . He carried me back across the stream and constantly was asking me if I had any sharp pains or should we turn around. . . . I said No, I'm fine—just a little tired, just enjoying the hike. And as we were approaching back around the curve, I guess, close to the cabin . . . [he] said, "I think I'll go up through this wooded brush and see if I can get a little bit closer and maybe get some good grizzly pictures. . . . " I said—you know, I wasn't about to stop him . . . that's what he loves to do—and I said I'll just walk back to the truck and wait, and that was around 5:00 p.m.

He knew he had plenty of daylight time. . . . It was really, really warm, like I said, on that exposure, when we spotted the grizzly, because she stopped and rested under a tree, looking for some shade, and the cubs were kind of just playing. . . . And so I went back, I might have dozed a little bit, I just sat up in the cab and listened to the radio, and I think it was really [around] 7:30 that [I] just kind of started [worrying].

[By] 8:30 [p.m.] it's starting getting dusk, and he should be here soon—and 9:00 it was pretty dark, but maybe he got right to the edge of the trail and he would be there shortly after dark. At 10:00 I said I'd wait till 10:15, and start looking for someone to contact, and remembered passing the Walton Ranger Station on the way in, assumed that might be the closest contact and phone.

She arrived at the Walton Ranger Station, where rangers immediately responded to her plea for help, organizing a search party and requesting helicopter assistance. Of course, the light was gone and the night had arrived.

"[I] received a phone call from Ranger [redacted] at Walton who was reporting an overdue hiker in the Fielding area," wrote the Reporting Ranger (R/R) [name redacted] in the "Supplementary Case/Incident Record," dated May 2, 1987. The time was "approximately 2345 hours [11:45 p.m.] on 4/25/87."

It was decided that [name redacted] would hike into the Fielding patrol cabin and conduct a hasty search, taking proper precautions in bear country. R/R held briefings for the Flathead Co. Sheriff and dog teams as well as NVSAR [search and rescue]. The NPS Command trailer was dispatched to the scene to serve as a field command post. A radio relay was also established at the Walton Ranger Station to relay radio traffic between the search area and park headquarters.

"Requesting [name redacted] to Fielding to stay with wife," the Radio Transmission Log KOE 729, Walton Ranger Station noted on April 26. The time was now 1:45 a.m. Finally daylight returned. At 9:00 a.m. three armed rangers set out to find Chuck Gibbs.

"We departed from the point last seen . . . and conducted a coarse [rough] grid, hasty search up the southwest flank of Elk Mountain in an effort to cut sign [spot evidence] of the victim and/or sow grizzly and cubs," wrote Ranger [redacted] in the Supplementary Case/Incident Record. The April 30 report continues:

We spaced ourselves approximately 50 meters apart and kept ourselves intervisible [keeping each in sight of the other]. The perimeter of our search area was marked with yellow flagging. We were delayed twice to allow Flathead County Sheriff Dept. search dog handlers to establish their search area, and then continued our search.

At approximately 1510 hrs [3:10 p.m.] at the 5,900-foot level on the southwest flank of Elk Mountain, I observed the body of the victim lying in a supine position in open ground approximately 20 meters to my right (east). I shouted for assistance from Rangers [redacted], and after they covered my advance with shotguns, I approached the body. I observed the body of a male matching the description of Gibbs and radioed the command post that I had an apparent Code 10–50f [fatality].

There was no pulse or respirations present on the body and rigor mortis had set in on the extremities. The pupils were fixed and dilated. The body had numerous frontal area wounds which appeared to have been inflicted by a bear. There were no drag marks or indication of a struggle at the location of the body.

Evidence at that location indicated that the victim had been dragged out of a tree and had attempted to fend off the bear while facing it. Wounds on the body were exclusively on the front of the body. Ranger [redacted] located the victim's blue camera bag containing extra camera body and lenses approximately 200 meters downslope. It appeared to have been purposefully placed there by the victim. The body location and apparent attack site were marked and secured. The victim was airlifted from the site by a Malmstrom Air Force Base helicopter. Ground teams cleared from the scene at approximately 1730 hrs [5:30 p.m.].

Evidence—Clothing: The victim was wearing tan trousers, a blue and tan checked flannel long-sleeved shirt, a gray undershirt with red sleeves, blue/gray socks, a brown leather belt, and LaCrosse hightopped leather/rubber boots with round nubbed rubber soles. A black nylon/cordura shoulder holster was on the body but did not contain a weapon. It was under the victim's back and left side and also contained an empty and unsnapped leather ammunition dump pouch. . . .

I observed no bear tracks, scat or other sign in the immediate vicinity of the body. The victim's .45 semiautomatic Colt and camera were found at the apparent attack site on the ground. There were no spent bullet casings found at the scene. There was no ammunition recovered from the immediate vicinity of the body. . . . Photographs of the body and the scene were taken on-site.

On April 27, Ranger [redacted] "met with Mrs. Gibbs at the Bear Creek Ranch and conducted an interview, recorded on cassette tape, regarding events leading up to the incident." The ranger continues in his Supplementary Case/Incident Record, dated 4/30/87: "I then escorted Mrs. Gibbs and her friends to the trailhead per Mrs. Gibbs's request."

On April 28, "At about noon . . . [name redacted] called me to advise that [two names redacted] had searched the incident scene with a metal detector with negative results." No bullets or bullet casings were found. Although the gun recovered did not have a recently cleaned barrel, it was found that it was unlikely that the gun had been fired (and so neither the sow nor cubs had run off injured by a gunshot).

"I conducted a patrol of the Autumn Creek Trail and found only one fresh bear track toward the lower end of the trail," wrote [redacted] in his Supplementary Case/Incident Record of April

30. "At noon I met with [three names redacted] and reported additional findings at the scene, including blood-soaked tree limbs approximately 18 feet up a tree and evidence of blood locations on the ground around the scene not noted before."

On May 14, a cause of death was reported, which the coroner gave as "hemorrhaging." The "Nature of Incident" was listed as "DEATH/ ACCIDENTAL Bear Mauling." What did the exhaustive investigation find? On May 14, a "Summary of Investigation" was prepared by a Park employee, whose name was redacted. The time was given as 3:10 p.m. on April 26.

Mr. Gibbs's body was found at about the 5,900-foot level on the south aspect of Elk Mountain, about 3/4 mile and 1,100 feet above the point last seen on the Fielding Trail. Mr. Gibbs was the apparent victim of a fatal bear mauling incident.

Evidence found at the scene included a blood trail leading directly downhill for about 150 feet from the base of two trees to Gibbs's location. Scattered about the base of these two trees were found a semiautomatic pistol with five rounds in the magazine and one round in the chamber (cocked and off safety); a roll of exposed film; two folding knives; a camera with a 400 mm lens attached; six unspent rounds of ammunition; two cough drops and two cough drop wrappers; and a Boot print of Chuck Gibbs (left boot) sketched from track on the Fielding Trail, April 26, 1987. Sketches of fresh bear tracks found on snowfield on April 26, approximately one-half mile southwest of the fatality site.

Another blood trail was found between the base of the most northerly tree ("tree #1") for about 20 feet east and at a right angle (across slope) to the fall-line. In tree #1 several freshly broken branches were found up the tree to a height of 20 feet. Bear claw marks were found up the tree to a height of 14 feet. Hair from a bear was also found at 14 feet. A blood-soaked branch (not broken) was found at 16 feet up the tree. Several broken branches, green and dead, were found at the base of [the] tree, some stained with blood.

Approximately 150 yards below the body (200 yards below tree #1) was found a camera bag at the base of a tree. The bag was upright, closed, and contained a camera body, binoculars, film, lenses, and camera filters.

Two rolls of exposed film found at the scene (roll in camera and roll found at the base of tree #1) were processed by Kodak laboratories, and 40 slide photographs taken by Mr. Gibbs in the hours leading up to the time of his death were obtained. Thirty-nine of the photographs are of grizzly bear(s) and one photograph is of an Amtrak train passing "Blacktail Station" near the Fielding Trailhead.

On 5/13/87 rangers returned to the scene of the incident with prints of Mr. Gibbs's photographs and a camera with a 400 mm lens to determine Mr. Gibbs's location when each photograph was taken. Mr. Gibbs's locations were determined in all but three places with very high confidence.

Results indicate that Mr. Gibbs photographed the bears from eight different locations on Elk Mountain, from a standing position, in the open (not concealed by rock or vegetation). His first position was near the tree where the camera bag was found, and photographs taken here are believed to have been taken with a lens other than 400 mm. The seven other photograph positions were within 150 feet of the incident scene (about 200 yards uphill from the first position). The farthest distance measured between

Mr. Gibbs's positions and the bears was 280 feet; the closest was 168 feet, and was at the last photograph taken.

What happened to the golden-tan mother grizzly and her three golden-tan cubs? A "Report of Accident/Incident" under the letterhead "US Department of the Interior, Safety Management Information System," stated the following: "Corrective action taken or planned. At this time it is believed the attack was provoked by the possible surprise encroachment on a grizzly bear. No action taken or planned at this time pending further investigation."

Would Chuck have agreed?

Chuck's wife, on the day after his disappearance, told Ranger [redacted] that "Her husband had a great admiration for grizzly bears, and would not have wanted the bear responsible for his death to be killed." (See Supplementary Case/Incident Record dated May 10, 1987, by Ranger [redacted] in Case Incident Record Number 870092.)

The four grizzlies are gone now, vanishing into the backcountry of Glacier Park. Their photographs remain.

The wife of Chuck Gibbs described that day of April 25, before the tragedy occurred, as a "beautiful afternoon." Where Chuck was found on Elk Mountain, a large cairn of rocks now stands.

CHAPTER FOUR

The Grizzly: Our Greatest Wild Animal

Enos A. Mills

(Excerpted from Our Greatest Wild Animal, *Houghton Mifflin, 1919.)*

THE SCIENTIFIC NAME FOR THE GRIZZLY, URSUS ARCTOS HORRIBILIS, *certainly gets your attention. And while the word* horribilis *fits the bear's actions at times, the story of the grizzly is much more involved and complicated than any one word can describe.*

It would make exciting reading if a forty-year-old grizzly bear were to write his autobiography. Beginning with the stories from his mother of the long and exciting journey of his ancestors from far-off Asia and of her own struggle in bringing up her family, and then telling of his own adventurous life and his meetings with men and with other animals, he could give us a book of highly dramatic quality.

In the grizzly bear we have the leading animal of North America, and one who might well be put at the head of the wildlife of the earth. He has brain and brawn. He is self-contained and is prepared for anything. He makes an impressive appearance. He looks capable. He has bulk, agility, strength, endurance, repose, courage, enthusiasm, and curiosity. He is a masterful fighter if forced to defend himself.

But, a century ago, fifty years ago, or to-day, one could ramble the grizzly's territory in safety—unless attempting to kill a grizzly. The grizzly objects to being killed. If he is surprised or crowded so that he sees no escape, if the cubs are in danger or the mother thinks they are, or if the bear is wounded, there will be a fight or a retreat; and the grizzly will not be the one retreating. Almost every animal—wild or domestic—will fight if cornered or if he thinks himself cornered.

Before the days of the repeating rifle the grizzly boldly wandered over his domain as absolute master; there was nothing for him to fear; not an aggressive foe existed. But, being ever curious, he hastened to examine whatever interested him. The novel outfit of Lewis and Clark, which appears to have attracted unusual attention even from frontier people, must naturally have aroused the highest pitch of interest in the numbers of bears congregated in places along the river. There were boats of odd type,—some with sails,—strange cargoes, men in picturesque accoutrements, and even a colored man. The frequent close approaches which the bears made in trying to satisfy their curiosity caused Lewis and Clark to think them ferocious.

But is the grizzly bear ferocious? All the firsthand evidence I can find says he is not. Speaking from years of experience with him my answer is emphatically, "No!" Nearly every one whom a grizzly has killed went out with the special intention of killing a grizzly. The majority of people who hold the opinion that he is not ferocious are those who have studied him without attempting to kill him; while the majority who say that he is ferocious are those who have killed or attempted to kill him.

During the greater part of my life I have lived in a grizzly bear region. I have camped for months alone and without a gun in their territory. I have seen them when alone and when with hunters, in Colorado, Utah, Arizona, Mexico, Wyoming, Montana, Idaho, Washington, British Columbia, and Alaska. I have spent weeks trailing and watching grizzlies, and their tracks in the snow showed that they often trailed me. They frequently came close, and there were times when they might have attacked me with every advantage. But they did not do so. As they never made any attack on me, nor on any one else that I know of who was not bent on killing them, I can only conclude that they are not ferocious.

Once I was running down a Wyoming mountainside, leaping fallen fire-killed timber, when suddenly I surprised a grizzly by landing within a few feet of him. He leaped up and struck at me with sufficient force to have almost cut me in two had the blow landed. Then he instantly fled. This, however, was not ferocity. Plainly he thought himself attacked and struck in self-defense.

There are many naturalists and frontiersmen who affirm from first-hand experience that the grizzly is not ferocious, and following are given a number of quotations from a few of these men.

John Muir, who spent about forty years in the wilderness home of the grizzly bear, from 1868 to 1912, usually camped alone and never carried firearms. He has repeatedly called attention in his books to the wilderness as a place of safety, and has mentioned that grizzly bears are masters in attending to their own affairs; also that bears have effectively suggested to wilderness visitors to do likewise. In *Our National Parks* Muir says:—

In my first interview with a Sierra bear we were frightened and embarrassed, both of us, but the bear's behavior was better than mine. . . . After studying his appearance as he stood at rest, I rushed forward to frighten him, that I might study his gait in running. But, contrary to all I had heard about the shyness of bears, he did not run at all; and when I stopped short within a few steps of him, as he held his ground in a fighting attitude, my mistake was monstrously plain. I was put on my good behavior, and never afterwards forgot the right manners of the wilderness.

Muir also says, in *Steep Trails*:—

> There are bears in the woods, but not in such numbers nor of such unspeakable ferocity as town-dwellers imagine, nor do bears spend their lives in going about the country like the devil, seeking whom they may devour. Oregon bears, like most others, have no liking for man either as meat or as society; and while some may be curious at times to see what manner of creature he is, most of them have learned to shun people as deadly enemies.

Mr. William H. Wright spent most of his time from 1883 to 1908 as a hunter of wild animals, and especially as a hunter of the grizzly. In addition to being an observer of exceptional care while hunting and trapping, he spent some years in photographing grizzlies. He first studied them in order to hunt them successfully; then laid aside his rifle and hunted them to study them. From full acquaintance with the grizzly Mr. Wright declares that he is not ferocious. He offers the following comment concerning his curiosity—a trait which early explorers mistook for ferocity:

> We know now that the grizzly is chock-full of curiosity, and that one of his habits is to follow up any trail that puzzles or interests him, be it of man or beast. This trait has been noted and misconstrued by many. . . . So often have I seen this curiosity and proved it to be innocent that I have no fear whatever of these animals when indulging in this weakness of theirs. Time and again I have allowed one to approach within a few yards of me, and no calm observer who had watched a bear defying his own caution to satisfy his own inquisitiveness could mistake the nature of his approach.

Drummond, the botanist, had numerous experiences with grizzlies in the Rocky Mountains in 1826. He was familiar with their curiosity. He says that often they came close and stood up to look at him. But if he made a noise with his specimen-box, or "even waved his hand," they ran away.

James Capen Adams hunted and trapped big game from 1849 to 1859 in California and along the Pacific Coast. He captured numerous grizzlies, both old and young, and literally domesticated them. He discusses their characteristics at length. He knew them intimately, and in summing them up after years of close association he says of the grizzly, "He did not invite combat."

Kit Carson, another frontiersman of long experience with grizzlies, in writing of them does not call them ferocious.

Dr. W. T. Hornaday knows the grizzly in the wilds and has long and intimately known him in the zoo. In *The American Natural History* Dr. Hornaday has the following:

> I have made many observations on the temper of the Grizzly Bear, and am convinced that naturally the disposition of this reputedly savage creature is rather peaceful and good-natured. At the same time, however, no animal is more prompt to resent an affront or injury, or punish an offender. The Grizzly temper is defensive, not aggressive; and unless the animal is cornered, or—thinks he is cornered—he always flees from man.

The early explorers were warned by the Indians that the grizzly was "an awful and ferocious animal." All the early writers had the preconceived belief that the grizzly was ferocious. Many of these writers never saw a grizzly, but wrote down as fact the erroneous conclusions of the Indians. The few writers who did see a grizzly evidently judged him largely from these preconceived ideas. Even Lewis and Clark describe a number of the grizzly's actions and call him ferocious when the very actions which they describe simply show him as being curious, interested, or, at worst, excited at their strange appearance. They misinterpreted what actually happened.

A few sentences from Audubon well illustrate the wrought-up frame of mind of many hunters and authors when hunting or writing about the grizzly. Audubon says:—

> While in the neighborhood where the grizzly bear may possibly be hidden, the excited nerves will cause the heart's pulsations to quicken if but a startled ground squirrel run past, the sharp click of the lock is heard and the rifle hastily thrown to the shoulder before a second of time has assured the hunter of the trifling cause of his emotion.

This suggests emotion but not accuracy.

In summing up the animals of the North and West in 1790, Edward Umfreville wrote of the "red and the grizzle bear" that "their nature is savage and ferocious, their power dangerous, and their haunts to be guarded against."

In 1795 Sir Alexander MacKenzie recorded the following:

> The Indians entertain great apprehension of this kind of a bear, which is called the grisly bear, and they never venture to attack it except in a party of least three or four.

Henry M. Brackenridge, author of *Views of Louisiana*, wrote the following from hearsay:

> This animal is the monarch of the country which he inhabitates. The African lion or the Bengal tiger are not more terrible than he. He is the enemy of man and literally thirsts for human blood. So far from shunning, he seldom fails to attack and even to hunt him. The Indians make war upon these ferocious monsters with ceremonies as they do upon a tribe of their own species, and, in the recital of their victories, the death of one of them gives the warrior greater renown than the scalp of an enemy. He possesses an amazing strength, and attacks without hesitation and tears to pieces the largest buffalo.

The grizzly was introduced to the world by Governor DeWitt Clinton of New York, who appears to have taken his information from the Journal of Lewis and Clark. In the course of an address before the Literary and Philosophical Society of New York City in 1814, he completely misinterpreted the real character of the grizzly and popularized a number of errors that not only were believed then but have survived to this day. The real grizzly is a distinguished character; but the grizzly as commonly described by tongue and story—well, "there ain't no such animal."

Governor Clinton in discussing the work in store for the coming naturalists said, "There is the white, brown, or grizzly bear, the ferocious tyrant of the American woods—it exists, the terror of the savages, the tyrant of all other animals, devouring alike man and beast and defying the attacks of a whole tribe of Indians." Few people realize to what extent these inaccurate words have discouraged outdoor life and how enormously they have contributed to the output of fictitious nature writing.

The Indians had a profound respect for the fighting efficiency of the grizzly. When one of them killed a grizzly he triumphantly wore the claw as a medal for rare bravery. The grizzly has a head and a hide that the Indian could rarely penetrate with either an arrow or a spear. We may readily believe that the grizzly defied the attacks of "a whole tribe of Indians," as Governor DeWitt Clinton said. He would defy a whole tribe of Indians or a score of white men with similar weapons to-day. So, too, would the elephant, the African lion, or the tiger.

With the rifles used at the time of Lewis and Clark it was necessary for the hunter to approach close to the bear that the bullet might have sufficient velocity to penetrate a vital spot. The rifles being only single-shot, the hunter was exposed to the assault of the bear in case his aim missed or the shot was ineffective. It is not surprising that in most cases those attempting to kill the grizzly either were overpowered by him or succeeded only through force of numbers and with the loss of some of the assailants. But the ability of the grizzly to withstand such attacks and to defend himself has been confused with ferocity.

The grizzly is a fighting-machine of the first order and with the weapons of two or three generations ago he often sold his life most dearly. In a short time the grizzly had the reputation of being a terrible fighter, and along with this he was given the reputation of being ferocious—of being an awful hunter of man. For the grizzly to repel effectually those who went out to attack him is a very different thing from his going out to hunt and to attack people who were not molesting him. This latter he has never done.

The words of Umfreville, MacKenzie, Brackenridge, Clinton, and Lewis and Clark bring out strongly that the grizzly is a fighter, formidable, perhaps unequaled. Their opinion on this point is supported by ample first-hand testimony down through the years, from all over the grizzly territory. But it has not been established that the grizzly is ferocious, is seeking to kill. No, the grizzly does not look for a fight; he is for peace at almost any price.

The grizzly fights in self-defense; men do the same. A man is not criminal for fighting in self-defense; neither is a grizzly. For this self-defense fighting the grizzly should not be put in the criminal class. "The worm will turn," is an old saying. All animals fight in self-defense, some more quickly than others. Few ever succeed against man; the grizzly often does. Apparently, the effective self-defense of the grizzly is responsible for his criminal reputation.

It is common for those who believe that the grizzly is ferocious to believe also that he eats human flesh. There is no known instance of his having done so.

We are now hearing that the Alaska bears are especially ferocious. Yet, in Alaska at the present time, and for many years in the past, the bear trails are concealed as much as possible by being in the woods. This would prevent the bear on the trail being readily seen by man. Along the sea, where much bear food is cast ashore, the trails are not upon the open beach but some distance away behind the trees. The bears depend on scent to tell them if there is anything along the shore to eat. Both their trails and their daily life in Alaska conclusively show that their chief concern is to keep away from and out of sight of man.

The experience with bears in the Yellowstone Park demonstrates that the grizzly is not ferocious. The Park had a numerous grizzly population when it was made a wild-life reservation. The people who in increasing numbers visited the Park carried no firearms and they were not molested by the grizzlies. Yet grizzlies were all about. After some twenty years of this friendly association of people and grizzlies, a number of grizzlies, dyspeptic and demoralized from eating garbage, and annoyed by the teasing of thoughtless people, became cross and lately even dangerous. But these bears cannot be called ferocious. Eliminate the garbage-piles and cease harassing the bears, and they will again be friendly.

The grizzly bear has been a golden gift of the gods for the countless writers of highly colored alleged natural history. There is a type, too, of wild fiction-writers of the Captain Mayne Reid class whose thrilling stories of the grizzly and other wilderness animals are purely fictitious, and, though not even pretending to be fact, appear to have been taken seriously by thousands. So prolific and continuous has been the output of these writers that facts have been lost, and it is practically impossible for the average individual to know the real grizzly bear. This comes near to being the immortality of error. It is a national misfortune that the overwhelming majority of people should be imposed upon with erroneous natural history. The destiny of the human race is intimately tied up with nature, and for anyone to misunderstand the simple facts which unite us with nature is to be out of harmony with the whole scheme of things. An accurate knowledge of natural history has an important place in guiding the judgments of our race.

Because of their intimate knowledge of the grizzly bear, James Capen Adams, William H. Wright, and Philip Ashton Rollins admired this animal. It would be a glorious thing if everyone appreciated the real character of the grizzly bear. A changed attitude toward him—the great animal of the outdoors—might cause the wilderness to appeal to all as a friendly wonderland.

CHAPTER FIVE

On Dangerous Ground

Lamar Underwood

WHEN I FIRST WROTE THIS CHAPTER OF MY NOVEL ON DANGEROUS Ground *(1989), I wanted to emphasize what I considered to be the most dangerous situation in all the outdoors: a grizzly bear on a kill. Since I wrote this tale, which was republished in my book* Classic Survival Stories (2004), *grizzly bears defending their kills have made many internet and newspaper headlines. The fact that I have chosen a story of my own may seem arrogant. Forgive me, if you feel that way, for I have not included the tale for any personal gain or satisfaction but for one reason only: I think most readers will enjoy it a great deal. If that explanation is not good enough, then perhaps one of today's common quips will suffice: I did it because I could.*

The four rainbow trout finned easily to hold themselves suspended in the current, their shadows wavering over the brown pebbly streambed at a place where the Toubok River curved from the dark canyon of a spruce forest and clattered sunlit and sparkling through a field of low alder bushes. Pointed into the flow, the fish did not see or detect the enormous grizzly as it slowly emerged from the shadowed timber and walked across the sandbar to the shoals behind their position. The great bear's muscles moved with fluid, rippling ease, so devoid of stiffness that the entire body seemed on the verge of collapse. Beneath the stumpy legs, the dry sand yielded to a depth of two inches as each footfall silently recorded the passage of the massive 1,500-pound creature. Its front feet, fifteen inches long by ten wide, bore claws that curved downward over the last half of their six-inch length. The rear feet were not as wide, their claws shorter. Tiny ears, a broad shelving forehead, and burly snout gave the bear's face a dog-like appearance. The deeply dished eyes were devoid of malevolence, innocently unexpressive. Thicker and wider than the head itself, the neck led back to the prominent hump that seemed to float, unattached to the rest of the body, as the creature walked, the light upstream breeze stirring the outer frosting of silver hair and the dark brown pelt beneath.

When he reached the edge of the current, the grizzly waddled into the flow without pausing, heading directly across the rocky shoals. The trout shot upstream into a deeper pool, splinters of light as they flared through the clear water. Across the stream, the grizzly paused to shake itself. His legs and underbelly blurred with motion as luminous mist flew from the soaked fur. In a moment, he went on. Shouldering through the border of alders that grew down to the water's edge, he headed downstream.

As the great bear walked along the river, his presence had an immediate impact on the rhythm of the late-afternoon life sustained by the stream. On a hillside across the river, pine squirrels saw the bear and began to chirr in scolding, nervous alarm. A pair of ravens watched the beast approach, then flapped away, croaking as they flew. Peering from the uppermost snag of a lightning-killed white spruce, an osprey saw the bear wade directly through the bay-like depression where it had been fishing. The bird lifted into the air, caught a thermal, and circled away downstream. A hen mallard and a drake, floating on the current, bounced straight up and curved away over the spruce tops, their wings whispering.

All day the great bear had foraged opportunistically while wandering through the river valley. Once, when he was crossing a saddle of talus rock that bridged two ridges on the slopes above the stream, he had detected the powerful odor of prey in the mixture of scents his amazing nose sorted from the mountain air: dank rock, moss and lichen, wildflowers, rotting snow, pumice and sand.

For several yards, he had coursed the trail over the stones like a bird dog, head down, wheezing as his nostrils flooded with scent. Rounding a rocky shoulder, he was enveloped by a cloud of odor the wind brought down from the ledges above. The bear looked up and instantly crouched into a stalk, as a band of Dall sheep ewes and lambs came into view, alert and tense, their superb vision focused on the menace before them. They watched, mesmerized for a moment, then bounded up the slope with a harsh rattling of hooves. The bear broke into a sprint for a few yards, then slowed and stopped as the weaving, bobbing forms disappeared over the ridge line. The grizzly watched the empty slope for a few moments, then turned and resumed his journey.

Later he spent two frustrating hours trying to dig a ground squirrel from its den. Barely larger than a mouse, the squirrel had screeched in mortal terror as the claws scratched and probed to within inches of its perch in a tunnel between two underground rocks. But the huge paws could not be forced into the tiny aperture. Finally, snorting with excitement, the grizzly began to dig for the tiny morsel. By the time he became bored with the pursuit and wandered on his way, the torn ground looked as if a bomb had struck.

Since copulating with a sow and then immediately leaving her two weeks before, the grizzly had become increasingly obsessed with feeding. He had been with the female for ten days, following the steady, aimless wanderings that are part of the great bears' courtship rituals, and the experience had burned away the last of the winter fat he had brought from his many weeks of semi-hibernation. Now his instincts had carried him down from the higher ranges to the fertile lower slopes, where he expected to find the tubers of wildflowers, seed pods, plant bulbs, and other growths that composed the greater part of his diet at this time of the year. There were pea vine roots to dig, horsetail and sourdock plants to chomp down. Also, another sense of need gripped the great bear, pulling him deeper into the river valley. Usually by this time every spring, the banks of the river had provided the special food that would satisfy the craving that gnawed at him. Carrion—a moose or caribou carcass, gift of the melting winter snows—would bring the strength and satisfaction the grizzly instinctively knew he needed. The memory of such rich feeding could not be obliterated by a diet of plants, and for days the grizzly's instincts had held him close to the river. Sometimes he wandered the nearby ridges for a while, but he always came back to the current, searching expectantly along the brushy shoreline.

The great bear continued downstream, slipping in and out of the alders like some enormous shadow. When the thicket began to thin, the grizzly stopped. Across a wide expanse of muskeg that came down to the edge of the stream, open country stretched away to a distant line of timber. Closer, on one side of the muskeg, a line of willows gave way to a belt of spruce on high ground.

The bear moved into the thicket, stopped again. In every direction, the willows had been heavily browsed, the ground scarred and trampled. The scent of the beast that had fed there permeated the air like fog. The bear stepped gingerly ahead, drinking in the smell, seeking a source for the diffused odor.

Twenty yards to one side, a thick clump of brush exploded with noise and movement. A cow moose crashed through the brush and headed across the clearing, trotting in a ragged gait. Instantly the grizzly charged.

The moose bolted in panic, nostrils flaring, eyes bulging wildly. She looked back over her shoulder just as a paw smashed into the side of her neck, breaking it with a crack that resounded over the bear's roar and the collision of the massive bodies. The bear's bulk hurtled into the cow's shoulder, breaking bones and battering muscle and sinew into pulp. One of the cow's front legs snapped under the impact, and she was thrown forward and to one side, landing on her shoulder, her head and neck flopping limply as they thudded to the ground. The grizzly bit into the flesh, sinking his fangs deep into the blood-spurting neck, shaking his head as he tightened his grip.

Gradually, the grizzly sensed the lack of movement in his prey and relaxed his hold. He stood for a moment, watching the carcass. The cow's eyes stared ahead, wide and empty, the light inside extinguished since the initial blow to the neck.

The great bear circled, sniffing and watching. Finally, he bit into the base of the neck, braced his massive shoulders, and began to pull the cow along the ground. Despite his brute strength, the grizzly could only move the body a foot or so in one continuous pull. Stopping periodically to look around and sniff the air for intruders, then bending down to gain a new purchase on his prize, the bear worked for over an hour to move his kill twenty yards from the willows. The opening where he finally stopped was closer to the spruce trees and the river but was almost identical to the spot where the moose had been struck down.

For some strange reason, however, the grizzly's instincts were satisfied now. His paws resting on the carcass, he lifted his nose, inspecting the light currents of air.

Finally, he began to feed.

A pair of magpies watched from a nearby branch, keeping their distance for now but knowing their turn would come.

"I'd feel a whole lot better about leaving you here if you'd take this." The pilot clicked back the hammer of the long-barreled .44 magnum revolver. "Hell, I'll even show you how to use it." He held the gun with a two-handed combat grip, steadied his feet on the pontoons of the floatplane, and aimed across the water.

To Sam Larkin, the metallic snap of the hammer falling on an empty chamber seemed a strange sound above the lapping of the gentle waves against the rocks. He glared silently at the plane as it floated over the sun-dappled shallows, some ten yards from the level slab of stone where he and his backpacks had just been put ashore. From far down the lake, the call of a loon echoed through the stillness. The cry was at once lilting and plaintive, a cry of wildness and solitude. The pilot lowered the handgun, opened the action, and idly spun the empty cylinder. The holster belt that sagged from his waist was lined with blunt-nosed cartridges that gleamed dully. To Larkin, the idea of lugging that grim bulk and heaviness through the Alaska wilderness for the next ten days was too depressing to contemplate. He smiled at the pilot, trying to show appreciation for his offer.

"I'll be all right," Larkin said. "I've lived in New York City for seven years without a gun. That's more dangerous than being out here."

"No it ain't," the pilot answered.

Larkin studied the man's face for a sign of levity. The eyes were cold dark slits, the other features expressionless behind a heavy reddish beard and long hair that spilled from a baseball cap with a Cessna label on the front. Larkin suspected that the pilot was very young, but he could not be certain. Whatever his age, he had handled the plane well on the flight from Anchorage, setting the single-engined 182 on the small lake with a deftness and precision that Larkin had admired. Now the pilot had become an intruder. Larkin wanted him to be on his way.

"Wilderness grizzlies just want to be left alone," Larkin said. "They'll bugger off as long as you don't do something stupid, like surprise one."

"If this is your first trip to Alaska, how come you know so much about our bears?"

"I read a lot. I've been looking forward to this for a long time."

The pilot shrugged his shoulders. He unbuckled the gun, turned quickly, and eased gingerly along the pontoon to the cockpit. Larkin knelt on one knee and began checking the straps of his oversized backpack and a smaller shoulder pack.

The pilot carried a paddle as he came back to the front of the pontoon. Kneeling, he thrust the blade down against the brown-pebbled bottom and pushed hard to shove the plane out of the shallows. "You know," he called, "a lot of those writers have never seen a bear, 'cept in a zoo. What they write about is all made-up bullshit."

"Thanks for your help," Larkin called. "I'll be careful."

He could imagine what the pilot was thinking: this tenderfoot's gonna get his smart New York ass in deep-shit trouble. Larkin realized that almost everything about his appearance looked new and untested: his khaki trousers and long-sleeve cotton jersey, his packs, even his boyish, lightly tanned face. His blond hair was cut short and neat. The only marks of backcountry experience about him were his well-worn boots, with leather uppers, rubber bottoms, and heavy-lugged Vibram soles—a perfect combination for the springy tundra and swampy lowlands, as well as the harder ground along the slopes of the ridges.

The plane was floating in deeper water. The pilot could no longer touch the bottom with his paddle. He stood and shouted to Larkin.

"Okay, so don't surprise a grizzly. But, if you should happen to, do you know what to do?"

"Shout. Sing. Whistle. Anything to make noise and scare it way."

"No, that's all wrong!" The pilot waved his hand impatiently. "If you should happen up on a grizzly, say as close as I am to you right now, there's only one thing to do."

"What's that?" Larkin called, interested.

"The only thing you can do is to relax. Otherwise, you'll die all tensed up."

Larkin chuckled at the gag before he realized the pilot was not smiling.

"Rock Lake, ten days from now," Larkin called, getting back to business. "I'll be there."

"Don't eat all your food," the pilot shouted. "If the weather socks in, you'll have to camp at the lake till we can fly. Just sit tight."

The pilot climbed into the cockpit, slammed the door, and waved at Larkin as the electrical circuits hummed and the engine sputtered to life.

Larkin stood at the edge of the water and watched the plane taxi slowly downwind. Against the dark line of trees at the far end of the lake, the plane looked like a brightly painted toy. It made a slow U-turn and headed back toward Larkin, plowing quickly through the water. He could see white explosions of foam as the ship picked up speed. In a moment the roar of the engine was upon him and the pontoons were skimming the surface, throwing twin contrails of spray over their wakes. The plane rose slowly from the water and immediately leveled off, gathering speed. As the plane approached the shore it began to climb steeply and was still climbing as it roared overhead and out of sight beyond the spruce hillside behind the edge of the lake. Larkin looked at his watch. It was 8:00 p.m. here, midnight back in New York. He had left his Upper West Side apartment at 6:00 a.m. Now, eighteen hours later, he was on a trail deep in the Alaska Range.

Larkin looked out across the water, listening for the call of the loon. Light breezes stroked the surface into wavelets that shimmered in the sunlight. Along the shoreline, the water was dark and smooth in the shadows of the low hills cupping the lake. The silence was like some strange new sound that rang in the ears. Then the loon's cry danced across the water again. Somewhere nearby, a fish swirled. Larkin felt a surge of pleasure. He was alone but not lonely.

He pulled a map from a side pocket of his backpack. The act of unfolding the map and checking his position was a formality. The curving patterns of brown, green, and blue lines had been engraved in his mind during the countless hours he had spent poring over the map in anticipation of the trip.

On the map, his landing spot was a tiny dot squeezed by flowing contour lines that marked the surrounding hills. A line indicating a trail wiggled away from where he stood and brought his finger to the serpentine course of the Toubok River, which flowed out of the Alaska Range. After hiking upstream along the river for a week, he intended to cut cross-country to Rock Lake, where the float plane would pick him up. He expected to do some superb fishing and hiking while enjoying grand views and ideal campsites all along the way. He slipped the map back into the backpack and weighed his next move. There was no need to hurry; even after the sun dipped below the horizon, it would rise again before full darkness descended. The demands that usually made him pressed for time were behind him now. Out here, he would let events flow along at their own pace. He would enjoy the view for a bit before moving toward the river to find a campsite. Despite the long hours of his journey, he felt only exhilaration.

He opened a flap of the shoulder pack and reached inside for his binoculars. He sat down on the rock shelf where the barren stone was splashed with color; lichens formed filigrees of purple, doughnuts of green, mushroom bursts of orange.

Larkin raised his knees and leaned forward to steady his elbows as he lifted the glasses. The compact but powerful ten by forty lenses bit into the distance and pulled startling detail into view.

Green and bright in the evening sunlight, the surrounding forest of spruce, birch, and cottonwood stretched away toward the ramparts of the Alaska Range. The spruce on the lower slopes of the mountains gave way to gulches of misty-green alder that crept up the ridges for a distance, then disappeared into the grayness of rock ledges and shale saddles. Shadowed canyons gaped alongside the slanting ridges. Above, the snow line gradually began, first in scattered pockets where the sun never reached, then in blinding white couloirs flanked by hanging curtains of glacial ice. From this jumble of stone and icy blueness, the peaks themselves erupted into the skyline, hard-etched towers looming like sentinels on the edge of the earth.

Larkin lowered the binoculars, blinking. He felt he was on the brink of some secret Eden he would be the first to enter. No glitches on the trip, perfect weather on the trail. What more could he ask? The question produced a sudden stab of disappointment. Ted Walsh wasn't here. Sam's friend and companion of many trails and campfires had been forced to drop out of the trip, despite the fact that this trek was to have been the greatest of them all. "The finale of the carefree years," Walsh called it. Larkin was getting married later that summer.

The decision to press on alone had been an easy one for Sam. He had realized for some time that he enjoyed going solo in the wilderness.

God, he had brought a lot of stuff, Larkin thought as he reached for his backpack. He had treated himself to a new expedition-type pack with state-of-the-art features. The freeze-dried food and gear he felt he would need brought the unit to nearly sixty pounds. He braced his legs and swung the pack up to rest on an extended knee. With a quick and practiced move, he brought the load up and onto his back, pushing his arms through the shoulder straps. He staggered slightly as he wiggled into the contours of the pack's frame and reached for his waist belt. At that moment, Larkin could not help but think of the kidding he was being spared by Ted Walsh's absence. Walsh was the absolute master of reducing weight and bulk to gossamer. Ted's tricks—such as squeezing toothpaste from the tube and carrying it wrapped in light plastic—knew no limits. In his search for lightweight, efficient gadgets he was indefatigable.

Larkin swung the strap of the kit bag over his shoulder. The bag held his fishing gear: lures and flies, lightweight fly and spinning reels, and two pack rods that broke down into twelve-inch-long sections. He was ready to begin his journey. He looked at the lake and wondered if he would see it again. Perhaps with Susan, his bride to be, or with their children someday.

He turned to the trail, a faint trace that led up along the slope of the hillside and out of sight through the scattered spruce trees. Leaning forward against the heft of the pack, he started up the ridge. Behind him, the loon was still calling from far out on the lake.

A sudden itching sensation on the backs of his hands interrupted the pleasure Larkin was feeling. Frowning at his oversight, he slapped at the mosquitoes and reached into the shoulder pack to get some repellent.

Even paradise has its pests.

The willow thicket was quiet in the evening shadows. The magpies had ceased their quarrelling over the tidbits of flesh they could find on the ground where the grizzly had killed the moose. Smaller birds were hushed as well, leaving only the rustles of hares and ground squirrels and the swirls of rising fish. The pulse of the river world seemed to have vanished.

The carcass of the moose was almost unrecognizable now. Except for one section where a leg and hoof angled out crazily, and another where a brown patch of head lay exposed to the sky, empty baleful eyes jutting outward, the entire body was crudely covered with an assortment of brush and clumps of mossy tundra.

The great bear sprawled belly down on top of his handiwork, his legs splayed out, his head resting on a hump pushed up by the curve of the cow's shoulder. He was asleep.

Suddenly his eyes flickered, then opened wide. Without moving his head, he flared his nostrils and lifted his ears. He detected nothing that alarmed him. Then a trace of wind stirred through the willows and died away.

The grizzly slipped down from the kill without a sound and tensed into a crouch, his head thrust forward, his legs poised like springs. The sound that had awakened him was gone again. The still air held no scents that were new or threatening.

He heard the noise again, more distinct now, getting closer. Still there was no scent to send alarm through his twenty-ounce brain. But even without the message of scent, this grizzly's instincts told him the noise represented danger. He eased toward the side of the clearing, where the willows were thicker and a stand of birch trees began.

The grizzly vanished into the cover, a shadow moving within shadows.

The magpies flew down to the abandoned kill.

Sam Larkin was frustrated. He has passed up two decent campsites when he had first hit the river. Now, nearly an hour later, he was slogging through a swamp-like area where the current was hemmed in by a thick growth of alders. Forced to wade in the shallows to make any progress at all, he was sweating heavily and achingly tired. He had broken out the repellent again, and his face, hands, and hair reeked of the clammy paste of medicine and perspiration. Clouds of mosquitoes hovered in the still air. The sun had dipped behind the hills, and the breeze had died with it. Footing was difficult in the heavy shadows, and he had tripped twice, staggering and barely avoiding a headlong fall.

You're getting sloppy, Sam told himself. *This is exactly the kind of place where you have to worry about bears.* Everything he had read about the grizzly had stressed the point that the animal's relatively poor eyesight was more than offset by its superb hearing and remarkable nose. He remembered a Native American proverb from an article he had been reading on the plane only a few hours before. The pine needle fell in the forest. The eagle saw it fall; the deer heard it fall; the bear smelled it fall.

That was irony for you, Larkin thought. A grizzly on the cover of *In Wilderness* on the day I'm headed for Alaska. *In Wilderness* was a new national magazine Ted Walsh had edited since its inception a year ago. Difficulties at the magazine had knocked Walsh out of the trip with Sam, despite the fact that Walsh had planned the entire venture. One of the magazine's regular contributors lived on the Toubok, and Walsh had mapped out a trek that would include a surprise visit to the writer's cabin, four days' hike upstream. Even without Ted Walsh along, Sam had decided to stick to the original plan. He had always wanted to meet the writer, Jonathan Hill, whose article and photographs on the grizzly were the most recent in a series of pieces on Alaska.

Ahead, Sam could see a bend in the alders. The current was dark and smooth where it curved into view.

Okay, it's showtime, he told himself. He raised his voice in song. Bits and pieces of "Get Me to the Church on Time" filled the air as he waded on through the dark riffles.

He broke off in mid-note, laughing. His voice sounded absurdly loud and ridiculous above the murmur of the river.

"Instead of singing, I'll settle for talking to myself," Larkin mumbled. "It'll sound a helluva lot more pleasant. If there're any bears around here, I hope they hear me now!" Larkin called aloud. He shuddered at the alien sound of his own voice. "This is inane," he muttered.

Larkin sloshed on around the bend. The alders seemed to be thinning out, the terrain changing. Then he saw the river pouring straight at him from a stretch of open country where the muskeg plain and stands of spruce trees formed the horizon. Beyond a point of willows on the right bank, a ramp of dry, rocky soil slanted down from the higher ground.

Larkin's spirits soared. Camp at last!

The great bear crouched in the shadows, downwind of the willow thicket. The scent of the intruder flooded his nostrils now, triggering an instinctive force that compelled him to flee. But that force was only part of the complex emotions that stirred within him. The gamy odor of the moose kill made him confused and agitated.

He watched and waited.

Within moments, the scent of the intruder became overwhelming, raging toward the grizzly like a firestorm.

The smell of the moose kill mingled with the scent of the danger.

The meat provided strength, an instinctive sense of well-being.

The great bear was afraid. Yet he did not flee.

Suddenly he spotted movement. The willow branches shook, then parted.

The puny two-legged menace stood in the clearing, looking off toward the river.

Larkin had been trying to hurry. His boots made loud sucking noises as he trudged along the muddy bank where the willows grew down to the water. He paused to study the last thirty yards that separated him from the far side of the willow thicket and the beginning of the open ground. The willows seemed to be thinner up away from the bank of the river. He could see gaps in the clumps of bushes and a few scattered birches on beyond. He headed that way, expecting firmer ground.

He had to use his arms and hands to ward the thick branches from his face. The green limbs he shoved aside immediately whipped back into place, snagging on his packs. He pressed on through the tangle with dogged determination.

In a moment he broke into a clearing. To his right, away from the stream, the willows gave way to a stand of birches. Straight ahead he could see the tops of the spruces, which marked the beginning of the tundra plain. That was the spot where he wanted to make camp. The stillness was like a kind of vapor, and his breathing was labored, as if all oxygen had been squeezed out of the air.

He stepped ahead, then stopped, listening. He had heard something.

Faint and distant, the call of a loon broke through the stillness. Was that what he had heard? Terrific! Music for his first camp. There must be a lake somewhere over there. Loons were not river birds. He moved along a few paces, skirting the edges of a few willow clumps that loomed in the way.

Two magpies burst into flight from off to his left, squawking as they flapped on out over the river.

Larkin gasped, startled and shaken. A feverish chill swept over him, cutting through his general discomfort of fatigue, thirst, and hunger.

Come on, for Christ's sake, his thoughts urged. *Let's get to camp.* He started again, then paused in mid-step, staring at the place where the magpies had jumped, his mouth wide open.

The pile of brush that held his gaze was a haphazard mound of willow and spruce branches, bulging up waist high. In the middle of the tangle, the head of a moose stared at him with vacant unseeing eyes, like some strange, mounted trophy. A leg angled out of the brush to one side.

Larkin turned and looked around. The clearing was empty. The silence made the pounding of the blood in his temples feel like physical blows. He stood frozen to the spot, his mind trying to respond to a question he could not answer. *What in the name of God was going on?* An explanation—logical and compelling—came to him in a burst of clarity.

A hunter! A goddamn poacher! Killed the moose out of season and covered the carcass to hide it.

Adrenaline surged through his body. Random ideas shot through his mind and disappeared.

Poachers hid their kills from game wardens. The wardens used airplanes and helicopters. Where was the poacher? Was he hidden nearby right now, watching? Poachers had been known to commit murder!

Larkin looked around again. The silence and empty clearing mocked him in his panic. Then he heard the loon calling from the distant lake.

A lake! Was the poacher there? With an airplane?

Mesmerized by the vision before him, he took a tentative step toward the brush pile. Then another.

He heard a heavy nasal woof and in the same instant he felt his backpack explode and he was hurtling forward through the air. The breath burst from his lungs as his stomach and face hit the ground, and he was engulfed in a storm of roars and massive, twisting muscle and flesh. His mind was swept clear of thought, except for one word that flared again and again.

Grizzly!

Grizzly . . . a searing pain across his buttocks, then fangs sinking into flesh . . . grizzly . . . a paw crushing his shoulder, claws raking his neck . . . grizzly . . . a slobbering mouth biting at his head, the fangs skidding and tearing across the flesh . . . grizzly . . . his hands afire with pain, his hands that he flapped feebly over the back of his head for protection . . . grizzly . . . his face pushing down into the moss, seeking refuge and finally finding oblivion.

He was swimming up through a murky sea, unable to hold the surface, gasping and floating for a second, then going under again. Gradually this thread of consciousness strengthened, and the lucid realization that he was still alive finally came—not from growing strength but from pain.

He tried to hang on to a simple thought: *the bear is gone—but I must not move! I'll have to play dead in case the beast is still nearby.* His thoughts touched on the sources of his agony, one by one. His buttocks were ripped. His shoulder was smashed, and his neck felt hot and wet. His head throbbed with pain, and blood filled his right eye. He could be blind in that eye. He could not tell. His ears and hands were numb.

Despite his injuries, he was totally conscious now. He was coming back! His heart was strong, and he could live with the pain. Somehow, he was going to make it! What a story he would have to tell. He remained frozen to the ground, trying to listen, but hearing nothing except his own thoughts. The first nauseating waves of shock swept over him, eroding the little strength he had left.

Dimly, through a smear of blood over his left eye, he could see the bottom of a willow bush. Vague shapes that he knew were stuff from his backpack were strewn over the ground.

The backpack had saved him, that was for sure, he thought. Without it, the grizzly's first blow would have killed him.

He decided the bear must be gone. Perhaps he had been unconscious a long time. There was no way to tell. He moved his arm to bring his right hand down from the back of his head. Nothing happened. He tried to raise his hand so that he could see it. The bloody vision of his good eye cleared. His fingers were gone. The hand was a bloody stump of bones and torn flesh. Larkin screamed a shrieking, unearthly cry of terror and pain. His howl opened the earth. He was tumbling through the core of a roaring holocaust. Fangs found his face, and suddenly he was beyond any knowing. The great bear raked at the corpse with a final desultory swipe. He trotted to the side of the clearing and turned, crouching, watching. The body sprawled at the edge of the stream. A dark cloud of blood settled into an eddy, then was caught by the current and swept away. The loon was still calling from the distant lake. The sound was like the cry of something that had come from far away and was lost and afraid in the vastness.

CHAPTER SIX

Tundra Terror

Larry Mueller and Marguerite Reiss

(Excerpted from Bear Attacks of the Century, *Lyons Press, 2005.)*

FOR MOST PEOPLE, THE CHANCE TO SEE A LIVE POLAR BEAR DEPENDS ON having a good zoo nearby. Real, wild polar bears live in a far-north land of eternal ice and snow with few human villages or scientific outposts. When polar bears fail in their hunting and are starving, look out!

November 24, 1993.

"You fellows, stay alert." The security guard's words hung as a coda to the grim report that had just been delivered to the tiny population of Oliktok Point radar site: two polar bears were definitely roaming nearby, and a third had been seen in the vicinity earlier. It seemed the bears were drawn to the tiny outpost near the Beaufort Sea in northernmost Alaska by butchered bowhead whale meat that Inupiat Indians had stored near their fishing cabins, a mere three hundred yards away. Under ideal conditions, polar bears are able to smell food from twenty miles. With the bears already in the neighborhood, it was only a matter of time before they investigated cooking and garbage odors coming from the radar site as well.

Oliktok Point once housed dozens of military personnel as a link in the "DEW line," the United States' highly secret Distant Early Warning defense network guarding against over-the-pole attack from the Soviet Union. But with the thawing of the Cold War, the site crew was gradually pared down to a civilian staff of six, and security patrols had been eliminated.

Which is why sympathetic ARCO security guards from the nearby Kuparuk oil field frequently shared what they knew with Oliktok personnel.

Alex Polakoff, fifty-three, a hunter and thirteen-year veteran of the DEW line sites, but a recent arrival at Oliktok, took bears very seriously.

He had heard the horror stories. In 1985, a polar bear stuck its head through the kitchen window and had to be beaten back with a pool cue and an iron skillet. Another time, a driver delivering water from Prudhoe Bay was chased up a twenty-foot fuel tank ladder by a bear that surprised him from behind his truck. A site worker ran it off with a bulldozer. The next bear in camp was a grizzly. Back in 1990, near Point Lay radar site over on the Arctic Ocean, an Inupiat couple were confronted by an emaciated polar bear as they walked down a dark street. To secure his pregnant girlfriend's escape, the courageous twenty-eight-year-old man faced down the bear with his pocketknife. Fifty pounds of his body were eaten.

Alex's fellow Oliktok crewmember, mechanic Don Chaffin, fifty-five, was less concerned, almost cavalier, about polar bears. On one occasion Alex complained that the site's Chevy Suburban ought to be plugged into the living quarters building to keep the engine from freezing, arguing that he shouldn't have to risk a two-hundred-yard walk in the dark to the garage every time he was required to go to the airstrip in the middle of the night. Don chided him. "Alex is afraid the polar bears will get him." True. He was. Alex had also been frustrated by what he considered the lack of concern exhibited by both the Air Force, which owned the site, and Martin Marietta Services, which had contracted to run it.

Oliktok was built in the 1950s by sledding twenty-by-twenty-foot insulated aluminum modules into place, raising them onto pilings, and joining them end to end.

The site was composed of a "train" of these modules three hundred feet long in which the six men lived and worked. Despite the fact that a leaping polar bear can reach as high as sixteen feet, the windowsills were built only five feet off the floor. The six-foot pilings would raise the total height of the windows to ten or eleven feet above ground level. This safety cushion was somewhat compromised, however, by road gravel and snowdrifts that had accumulated alongside the building. Recent tracks under and along the building indicated that a bear had been looking in the outpost windows—windows that were snap-in, double-pane, and without security bars.

But what clinched the employees' status as bear bait in Alex's mind was the firearms rule. Each man could have a rifle, a shotgun, and a pistol for hunting and hiking, but they were kept in a locked gun safe and signed out as needed. The gun safe was mounted six inches off the floor between some lockers, its lock mounted so low it could be reached only by kneeling.

On November 26, a Nuiqsut villager killed one of the three bears that had been reported by the ARCO guard, and the sense of vigilance intensified around the compound. Within the next few days, biologist Richard Shideler was even invited to Oliktok to suggest means to better bear-proof the site. His recommendations: Increased outdoor lighting; doors that opened outward and closed against strong inside metal frames; bars over the windows; the removal of road material close to buildings; an end to storing garbage cans on the porch; chain-link skirting to prevent bears from hiding under buildings; perhaps even substantial iron cages surrounding outside doors so personnel could appraise the situation in safety before leaving. According to Shideler, no immediate actions were taken.

At 8:30 P.M. on the night of November 30, just hours after Shideler left, Don and support services worker Gary Signs, thirty-eight, were sitting on stools at the bar in the dayroom. Don was hunched over a crossword puzzle, his back to the window. On the bar's opposite side, Gary was working on a report when his peripheral vision caught a movement at the window. Polar bear! Don looked up, saw Gary staring past him, and swiveled toward the window.

Gary says Don slapped his magazine at the window to frighten off the bear, but Don recalls no such action. "Let's get out of here!" Gary yelled as he raced to the fire door leading to an adjacent room. The bear's head dropped below the three-foot-wide window frame as Don stumbled over a stool, trying to escape from behind the bar. Gary pulled the magnetic latch, stepped inside the doorway, and held the door for Don. After regaining his balance, Don sidestepped the stool and was rounding the bar when he heard glass explode. He looked back and yelled, "Oh, no!"

Like smashing ice to get at a seal, the polar bear leaped through the shattered window in a shower of glass, taking the frame with it. The giant animal landed beside Don and reared up in his terrified face. Don, still several feet from Gary in the doorway, grabbed the bear's muzzle in an attempt to protect himself. But the bear, standing a full foot taller than his six feet, stretched its head and neck forward and sunk its teeth into his jaw. With almost superhuman effort, he pushed against the bear's black nose and tore himself free for an instant, only to have his hand and arm severely bitten. As if experimenting with how best to kill its unusual prey, the bear began swatting its victim.

A terrible realization came to Gary as he watched this bloody encounter. The gun safe was in the next room, but the key was in an office two hundred feet in the opposite direction! He would have to scramble around the bear to get to it, and even if he made it, there was a good chance Don would be dead by the time he got back. Should he close the door and sacrifice Don to save himself and the other four?

The bear solved this dilemma by batting Don's 240-pound body through the doorway. Gary bolted for the opposite door, found a phone, dialed the public address system, and screamed, "Bear in building!" With nothing else at hand, he grabbed a fire extinguisher and rushed back. The bear was on top of Don now, biting at the back of his head.

Don could feel fangs grating on his skull. He saw flashes of lightning and felt a neck vertebra snap. He thought blood filling his right eye was blinding him, but, in fact, his eyeball was now resting on his cheek. He could only weakly cry, "Help me." Gary aimed the extinguisher's nozzle at the polar bear. A weak stream of water arced into its face. It raised its head and looked quizzically at Gary, and then merely resumed its grim work on Don. Mechanic Joe Peterson, thirty-seven, hadn't been able to make out the loud message over the public address system, but he heard a commotion and came running to investigate. Grabbing the extinguisher from Gary, he shouted, "Go get the gun case key!" Not a chance, thought Gary. The bear was now ten feet from the gun safe.

Even if he already had the key, it would be sure suicide to kneel that close to the bear while fiddling with the lock. Right now, he had to find something more persuasive than a dribbling fire extinguisher. He ran to the hallway and grabbed another extinguisher, this time a Halon model that would suck oxygen from the air and produce a distracting—he hoped—whoosh.

He came back into the gun safe room just in time to see Joe throw the empty extinguisher at the bear. Gary handed the second extinguisher to him and was running for a third when Alex arrived on the scene and was able to make out white fur through the thick haze of Halon fog.

Alex's hair stood on end and his strong fear of bears put him in a primal "fight or flight" mode. He raced back to his room and grabbed his fully loaded Mossberg 500. He had brought the gun from his previous work site, intending to store it in the gun safe, but had hid the gun in his room when he saw the unsafe conditions at Oliktok.

When he returned, he saw the bear jumping up and down on Don. He approached to within seven feet, squatted so that the slug's upward trajectory would be safely away from his unfortunate coworker, and fired into the bear's broad chest. No visible reaction.

He fired a second slug into the animal's chest. The bear rose from Don in slow motion and walked through a door into a small library room. Alex stepped to his left and fired two more slugs that he hoped would find the bear's chest. Of the four ounce-and-a-half slugs from the three-inch 12-gauge Magnum, one found the polar bear's heart. The animal dropped dead.

Gary and Joe got the key, retrieved their rifles, and hurried out to search for the third bear that had been sighted. Alex was left behind to make Don comfortable and try to keep him talking so that he wouldn't go into shock. "I'm cold," the badly mauled man mumbled, choking on his blood. Alex covered him with a blanket, slid a pillow under his head, and jammed an upholstered chair into the shattered window in an attempt to block the wind current carrying minus twenty- to thirty-degree temperatures. He had already called the ARCO oil site for an ambulance.

In the confusion, the paramedics thought the message was for them to pick up a corpse. They were leisurely driving down the road when Alex frantically waved them to the living quarters. A police officer from Prudhoe Bay, fifty miles away, arrived at 3:00 A.M. to check out "the shooting" and wanted to confiscate the shotgun. "The bear is lying over there—take a look," Alex said. "If you take my gun, take me, too. I'm not staying in this place without it."

Emergency room personnel at Providence Hospital in Anchorage, where Don was being flown, told Betty Chaffin that her husband had been shot in the back of the head and would be dead on arrival. That same misinformation—probably influenced by a missing patch of scalp at the back of Don's head—even had Alex worried when he heard it. Was it possible that a slug hit bone and deflected downward, killing his friend? It was 6:00 A.M. before a nurse called to say that Don was alive and, in fact, not shot.

Eventually, Don was left with a numb left leg, a numb right hand that drops things, five hundred stitches, and a hundred fifty staples in the back of his head, seven metal plates in his head, forty inches of scars in his head and face, and double vision (after several operations to his damaged right eye, it still tracks five degrees lower than the left). Although his medical bills are paid by workman's compensation, he claims he has lost all ability to earn a living.

A week after the attack, Richard Shideler found portable lights on loan from ARCO still at the radar site, but no recommended structural changes were initiated. He heard nothing further from either Martin Marietta or the Air Force. At some point, however, one-inch plywood was nailed over the windows.

On December 2, 1993, USAF and Martin Marietta personnel visited the site and immediately relaxed the firearms rules: one firearm would be available in each wing. Gary Signs and Joe Peterson were given plaques and commended for bravery. In a printed reprimand from Martin Marietta, R. E. Cunningham, the manager of communications, electronics, and meteorology acknowledged that had it not been for Alex's quick response, a far greater tragedy might have occurred. The balance of the letter, however, makes it clear that saving Don Chaffin's life, and perhaps his own and others' as well, was no excuse for violating project policy and procedures. Three days after the attack, Alex Polakoff left and never again worked at Oliktok Point again. He made Utah his home, but misses Alaska's vast wilderness.

CHAPTER SEVEN

Hunting the Grisly

Theodore Roosevelt

SEVERAL BIOGRAPHICAL WORKS ON ERNEST HEMINGWAY HAVE STRESSED that his boyhood idol was Theodore Roosevelt. The young Hemingway was captivated by Roosevelt's lifestyle in the great outdoors, a lifestyle vividly brought into consciousness by volumes of prose that described hunting adventures in the American west and in Africa. The prairies, plains, and mountains of the west and the savannahs and veldts of Africa, as described by Roosevelt, became the stuff of dreams for Hemingway, the ultimate destinations for the strenuous life he coveted.

Roosevelt's three Western hunting books, written and published from about 1884 to 1993, and his two-volume African Game Trails *(1910), appeared at a time when much of the prose being written in America was anything but sprightly. In many cases the word "stodgy" would not be unfair. Roosevelt's hunting stories, on the other hand, appeared with the snap, crackle, and pop of great descriptive writing, engaging and illuminating. The first book,* Hunting Trips of a Ranchman, *was published to critical acclaim.*

Roosevelt wrote his Western hunting books after taking on the life of a rancher in the Dakota Territory following the death of his wife in childbirth. The Hunting Trips of a Ranchman *was followed by* Outdoor Pastimes of An American Hunter *and* The Wilderness Hunter.

Today, the same prose that captivated young Ernest Hemingway and literary critics on both sides of the Atlantic is still as imminently readable as it ever was. His portraits of the land, the weather, the ranch life itself hold the reader hard. From the look and feel of riding a pony into the high country in a fall morning, to fighting to return to the ranch in a blizzard, Roosevelt's words carry the reader along in stories that focus strongly on hunting experiences, as opposed to portraits and descriptions of game animals. His are books of hunting stories, the kind of stories Roosevelt listened to and told himself by his thousands of campfires.

If out in the late fall or early spring, it is often possible to follow a bear's trail in the snow; having come upon it either by chance or hard hunting, or else having found where it leads from some carcass on which the beast has been feeding. In the pursuit one must exercise great caution, as at such times the hunter is easily seen a long way off, and game is always especially watchful for any foe that may follow its trail.

Once I killed a grisly in this manner. It was early in the fall, but snow lay on the ground, while the gray weather boded a storm. My camp was in a bleak, wind-swept valley, high among the mountains which form the divide between the headwaters of the Salmon and Clarke's Fork of the Columbia. All night I had lain in my buffalo-bag, under the lea of a windbreak of branches, in the clump of fir-trees, where I had halted the preceding evening. At my feet ran a rapid mountain torrent, its bed choked with ice-covered rocks; I had been lulled to sleep by the stream's splashing murmur, and the loud moaning of the wind along the naked cliffs. At dawn I rose and shook myself free of the buffalo robe, coated with hoarfrost. The ashes of the fire were lifeless; in the dim morning the air was bitter cold. I did not linger a moment, but snatched up my rifle, pulled on my fur cap and gloves, and strode off up a side ravine; as I walked I ate some mouthfuls of venison, left over from supper.

Two hours of toil up the steep mountain brought me to the top of a spur. The sun had risen, but was hidden behind a bank of sullen clouds. On the divide I halted, and gazed out over a vast landscape, inconceivably wild and dismal. Around me towered the stupendous mountain masses which make up the backbone of the Rockies. From my feet, as far as I could see, stretched a rugged and barren chaos of ridges and detached rock masses. Behind me, far below, the stream wound like a silver ribbon, fringed with dark conifers and the changing, dying foliage of poplar and quaking aspen. In front the bottoms of the valley were filled with the sombre evergreen forest, dotted here and there with black, ice-skimmed tarns; and the dark spruces clustered also in the higher gorges, and were scattered thinly along the mountain sides. The snow which had fallen lay in drifts and streaks, while, where the wind had scope it was blown off, and the ground left bare.

For two hours I walked onwards across the ridges and valleys. Then among some scattered spruces, where the snow lay to the depth of half a foot, I suddenly came on the fresh, broad trail of a grisly. The brute was evidently roaming restlessly about in search of a winter den, but willing, in passing, to pick up any food that lay handy. At once I took the trail, travelling above and to one side, and keeping a sharp look-out ahead. The bear was going across wind, and this made my task easy. I walked rapidly, though cautiously; and it was only in crossing the large patches of bare ground that I had to fear making a noise. Elsewhere the snow muffled my footsteps, and made the trail so plain that I scarcely had to waste a glance upon it, bending my eyes always to the front.

At last, peering cautiously over a ridge crowned with broken rocks, I saw my quarry, a big, burly bear, with silvered fur. He had halted on an open hillside, and was busily digging up the caches of some rock gophers or squirrels. He seemed absorbed in his work, and the stalk was easy. Slipping quietly back, I ran towards the end of the spur, and in ten minutes struck a ravine, of which one branch ran past within seventy yards of where the bear was working. In this ravine was a rather close growth of stunted evergreens, affording good cover, although in one or two places I had to lie down and crawl through the snow. When I reached the point for which I was aiming, the bear had just finished rooting, and was starting off. A slight whistle brought him to a standstill, and I drew a bead behind his shoulder, and low down, resting the rifle across the crooked branch of a dwarf spruce. At the crack he ran off at speed, making no sound, but the thick spatter of blood splashes, showing clear on the white snow, betrayed the mortal nature of the wound. For some minutes I followed the trail; and then, topping a ridge, I saw the dark bulk lying motionless in a snow drift at the foot of a low rock-wall, down which he had tumbled.

The usual practice of the still-hunter who is after grisly is to toll it to baits. The hunter either lies in ambush near the carcass, or approaches it stealthily when he thinks the bear is at its meal.

One day while camped near the Bitter Root Mountains in Montana I found that a bear had been feeding on the carcass of a moose which lay some five miles from the little open glade in which my tent was pitched, and I made up my mind to try to get a shot at it that afternoon. I stayed in camp till about three o'clock, lying lazily back on the bed of sweet-smelling evergreen boughs, watching the pack ponies as they stood under the pines on the edge of the open, stamping now and then, and switching their tails. The air was still, the sky a glorious blue; at that hour in the afternoon even the September sun was hot. The smoke from the smouldering logs of the campfire curled thinly upwards. Little chipmunks scuttled out from their holes to the packs, which lay in a heap on the ground, and then scuttled madly back again. A couple of drab-colored whisky-jacks, with bold mien and fearless bright eyes, hopped and fluttered round, picking up the scraps, and uttering an extraordinary variety of notes, mostly discordant; so tame were they that one of them lit on my outstretched arm as I half dozed, basking in the sunshine.

When the shadows began to lengthen, I shouldered my rifle and plunged into the woods. At first my route lay along a mountain side; then for half a mile over a windfall, the dead timber piled about in crazy confusion. After that I went up the bottom of a valley by a little brook, the ground being carpeted with a sponge of soaked moss. At the head of this brook was a pond covered with waterlilies; and a scramble through a rocky pass took me into a high, wet valley, where the thick growth of spruce was broken by occasional strips of meadow. In this valley the moose carcass lay, well at the upper end.

In moccasined feet I trod softly through the soundless woods. Under the dark branches it was already dusk, and the air had the cool chill of evening. As I neared the clump where the body lay, I walked with redoubled caution, watching and listening with strained alertness. Then I heard a twig snap; and my blood leaped, for I knew the bear was at his supper. In another moment I saw his shaggy, brown form. He was working with all his awkward giant strength, trying to bury the carcass, twisting it to one side and the other with wonderful ease. Once he got angry and suddenly gave it a tremendous cuff with his paw; in his bearing he had something half humorous, half devilish. I crept up within forty yards; but for several minutes he would not keep his head still. Then something attracted his attention in the forest, and he stood motionless looking towards it, broadside to me, with his fore-paws planted on the carcass. This gave me my chance. I drew a very fine bead between his eye and ear, and pulled trigger. He dropped like a steer when struck with a poleaxe.

If there is a good hiding-place handy it is better to lie in wait at the carcass. One day on the headwaters of the Madison, I found that a bear was coming to an elk I had shot some days before; and I at once determined to ambush the beast when he came back that evening. The carcass lay in the middle of a valley a quarter of a mile broad. The bottom of this valley was covered by an open forest of tall pines; a thick jungle of smaller evergreens marked where the mountains rose on either hand. There were a number of large rocks scattered here and there, one, of very convenient shape, being only some seventy or eighty yards from the carcass. Up this I clambered. It hid me perfectly, and on its top was a carpet of soft pine needles, on which I could lie at my ease.

Hour after hour passed by. A little black woodpecker with a yellow crest ran nimbly up and down the tree trunks for some time and then flitted away with a party of chickadees and nuthatches. Occasionally a Clarke's crow soared about overhead or clung in any position to the swaying end of a pine branch, chattering and screaming. Flocks of crossbills, with wavy flight and plaintive calls, flew to a small mineral lick nearby, where they scraped the clay with their queer little beaks.

As the westering sun sank out of sight beyond the mountains these sounds of birdlife gradually died away. Under the great pines the evening was still with the silence of primeval desolation. The sense of sadness and loneliness, the melancholy of the wilderness, came over me like a spell. Every slight noise made my pulses throb as I lay motionless on the rock gazing intently into the gathering gloom. I began to fear that it would grow too dark to shoot before the grisly came.

Suddenly and without warning, the great bear stepped out of the bushes and trod across the pine needles with such swift and silent footsteps that its bulk seemed unreal. It was very cautious, continually halting to peer around; and once it stood up on its hind legs and looked long down the valley towards the red west. As it reached the carcass I put a bullet between its shoulders. It rolled over, while the woods resounded with its savage roaring. Immediately it struggled to its feet and staggered off; and fell again to the next shot, squalling and yelling. Twice this was repeated; the brute being one of those bears which greet every wound with a great outcry, and sometimes seem to lose their feet when hit—although they will occasionally fight as savagely as their more silent brethren. In this case the wounds were mortal, and the bear died before reaching the edge of the thicket.

I spent much of the fall of 1889 hunting on the headwaters of the Salmon and Snake in Idaho, and along the Montana boundary line from the Big Hole Basin and the head of the Wisdom River to the neighborhood of Red Rock Pass and to the north and west of Henry's Lake. During the last fortnight my companion was the old mountain man, already mentioned, named Griffeth or Griffin—I cannot tell which, as he was always called either "Hank" or "Griff." He was a crabbedly honest old fellow, and a very skillful hunter; but he was worn out with age and rheumatism, and his temper had failed even faster than his bodily strength. He showed me a greater variety of game that I had ever seen before in so short a time; nor did I ever before or after make so successful a hunt. But he was an exceedingly disagreeable companion on account of his surly, moody ways. I generally had to get up first, to kindle the fire and make ready breakfast, and he was very quarrelsome. Finally, during my absence from camp one day, while not very far from Red Rock pass, he found my whiskey flask, which I kept purely for emergencies, and drank all the contents. When I came back he was quite drunk. This was unbearable, and after some high words I left him, and struck off homeward through the woods on my own account. We had with us four pack and saddle horses; and of these I took a very intelligent and gentle little bronco mare, which possessed the invaluable trait of always staying near camp, even when not hobbled. I was not hampered with much of an outfit, having only my buffalo sleeping bag, a fur coat, and my washing kit, with a couple of spare pairs of socks and some handkerchiefs. A frying-pan, some salt, flour, baking-powder, a small chunk of salt pork, and a hatchet, made up a light pack, which with the bedding, I fastened across the stock saddle by means of a rope and a spare packing cinch. My cartridges and knife were in my belt; my compass and matches, as always, in my pocket. I walked, while the little mare followed almost like a dog, often without my having to hold the lariat which served as halter.

The country was for the most part fairly open, as I kept near the foothills where glades and little prairies broke the pine forest. The trees were of small size. There was no regular trail, but the course was easy to keep, and I had no trouble of any kind save on the second day. That afternoon I was following a stream which at last "canyoned up," that is, sank to the bottom of a canyon-like ravine impassable for a horse. I started up a side valley, intending to cross from its head coulies to those of another valley which would lead in below the canyon.

However, I got enmeshed in the tangle of winding valleys at the foot of the steep mountains, and as dusk was coming on I halted and camped in a little open spot by the side of a small, noisy brook, with crystal water. The place was carpeted with soft, wet, green moss, dotted red with the kinnikinnic berries, and at its edge, under the trees where the ground was dry, I threw down the buffalo bed on the mat of sweet-smelling pine needles. Making camp took but a moment. I opened the pack, tossed the bedding on a smooth spot, knee-haltered the little mare, dragged up a few dry logs, and then strolled off, rifle on shoulder, through the frosty gloaming, to see if I could pick up a grouse for supper.

For half a mile I walked quickly and silently over the pine needles, across a succession of slight ridges separated by narrow, shallow valleys. The forest here was composed of lodge-pole pines, which on the ridges grew close together, with tall slender trunks, while in the valleys the growth was more open. Though the sun was behind the mountains there was yet plenty of light by which to shoot, but it was fading rapidly.

At last, as I was thinking of turning towards camp, I stole up the crest of one of the ridges, and looked over into the valley some sixty yards off. Immediately I caught the loom of some large, dark object; and another glance showed me a big grisly walking slowly off with his head down. He was quartering to me, and I fired into his flank, the bullet, as I afterwards found, ranging forward and piercing one lung. At the shot he uttered a loud, moaning grunt and plunged forward at a heavy gallop, while I raced obliquely down the hill to cut him off. After going a few hundred feet he reached a laurel thicket, some thirty yards broad, and two or three times as long which he did not leave. I ran up to the edge and there halted, not liking to venture into the mass of twisted, close-growing stems and glossy foliage. Moreover, as I halted, I heard him utter a peculiar, savage kind of whine from the heart of the brush. Accordingly, I began to skirt the edge, standing on tiptoe and gazing earnestly to see if I could not catch a glimpse of his hide. When I was at the narrowest part of the thicket, he suddenly left it directly opposite, and then wheeled and stood broadside to me on the hillside, a little above. He turned his head stiffly towards me; scarlet string of froth hung from his lips; his eyes burned like embers in the gloom.

I held true, aiming behind the shoulder, and my bullet shattered the point or lower end of his heart, taking out a big nick. Instantly the great bear turned with a harsh roar of fury and challenge, blowing the bloody foam from his mouth, so that I saw the gleam of his white fangs; and then he charged straight at me, crashing and bounding through the laurel bushes, so that it was hard to aim. I waited until he came to a fallen tree, raking him as he topped it with a ball, which entered his chest and went through the cavity of his body, but he neither swerved nor flinched, and at the moment I did not know that I had stuck him. He came steadily on, and in another second was almost upon me. I fired for his forehead, but my bullet went low, entering his open mouth, smashing his lower jaw and going into the neck. I leaped to one side almost as I pulled trigger; and through the hanging smoke the first thing I saw was his paw as he made a vicious side blow at me. The rush of his charge carried him past. As he struck he lurched forward, leaving a pool of bright blood where his muzzle hit the ground; but he recovered himself and made two or three jumps onwards, while I hurriedly jammed a couple of cartridges into the magazine, my rifle holding only four, all of which I had fired. Then he tried to pull up, but as he did so his muscles seemed suddenly to give way, his head drooped, and he rolled over and over like a shot rabbit. Each of my first three bullets had inflicted a mortal wound.

It was already twilight, and I merely opened the carcass, and then trotted back to camp. Next morning I returned and with much labor took off the skin. The fur was very fine, the animal being in excellent trim, and unusually bright-colored. Unfortunately, in packing it out I lost the skull, and had to supply its place with one of plaster. The beauty of the trophy, and the memory of the circumstances under which I procured it, make me value it perhaps more highly than any other in my house.

This is the only instance in which I have been regularly charged by a grisly. On the whole, the danger of hunting these great bears has been much exaggerated. At the beginning of the present century, when white hunters first encountered the grisly, he was doubtless an exceedingly savage beast, prone to attack without provocation, and a redoubtable foe to persons armed with the clumsy, small-bore, muzzle-loading rifles of the day. But at present bitter experience has taught him caution. He has been hunted for sport, and hunted for his pelt, and hunted for the bounty, and hunted as a dangerous enemy to stock, until, save in the very wildest districts, he has learned to be more wary than a deer, and to avoid man's presence almost as carefully as the most timid kind of game. Except in rare cases he will not attack of his own accord, and, as a rule, even when wounded his object is escape rather than battle.

Still, when fairly brought to bay, or when moved by a sudden fit of ungovernable anger, the grisly is beyond per-adventure a very dangerous antagonist. The first shot, if taken at a bear a good distance off and previously unwounded and unharried, is not usually fraught with much danger, the startled animal being at the outset bent merely on flight. It is always hazardous, however, to track a wounded and worried grisly into thick cover, and the man who habitually follows and kills this chief of American game in dense timber, never abandoning the bloody trail whithersoever it leads, must show no small degree of skill and hardihood, and must not too closely count the risk to life or limb. Bears differ widely in temper, and occasionally one may be found who will not show fight, no matter how much he is bullied; but, as a rule, a hunter must be cautious in meddling with a wounded animal which has retreated into a dense thicket, and has been once or twice roused; and such a beast, when it does turn, will usually charge again and again, and fight to the last with unconquerable ferocity. The short distance at which the bear can be seen through the underbrush, the fury of his charge, and his tenacity of life make it necessary for the hunter on such occasions to have steady nerves and a fairly quick and accurate aim. It is always well to have two men in following a wounded bear under such conditions. This is not necessary, however, and a good hunter, rather than lose his quarry, will, under ordinary circumstances, follow and attack it no matter how tangled the fastness in which it has sought refuge; but he must act warily and with the utmost caution and resolution, if he wishes to escape a terrible and probably fatal mauling. An experienced hunter is rarely rash, and never heedless; he will not, when alone, follow a wounded bear into a thicket, if by the exercise of patience, skill, and knowledge of the game's habits he can avoid the necessity; but it is idle to talk of the feat as something which ought in no case to be attempted. While danger ought never to be needlessly incurred, it is yet true that the keenest zest in sport comes from its presence, and from the consequent exercise of the qualities necessary to overcome it. The most thrilling moments of an American hunter's life are those in which, with every sense on the alert, and with nerves strung to the highest point, he is following alone into the heart of its forest fastness the fresh and bloody footprints of an angered grisly; and no other triumph of American hunting can compare with the victory to be thus gained.

These big bears will not ordinarily charge from a distance of over a hundred yards; but there are exceptions to this rule. In the fall of 1890 my friend Archibald Rogers was hunting in Wyoming, south of the Yellowstone Park, and killed seven bears. One, an old he, was out on a bare tableland, grubbing for roots, when he was spied. It was early in the afternoon, and the hunters, who were on a high mountain slope, examined him for some time through their powerful glasses before making him out to be a bear. They then stalked up to the edge of the wood which fringed the tableland on one side, but could get no nearer than about three hundred yards, the plains being barren of all cover. After waiting for a couple of hours Rogers risked the shot, in despair of getting nearer, and wounded the bear, though not very seriously. The animal made off, almost broadside to, and Rogers ran forward to intercept it. As soon as it saw him it turned and rushed straight for him, not heeding his second shot, and evidently bent on charging home. Rogers then waited until it was within twenty yards, and brained it with his third bullet.

In fact bears differ individually in courage and ferocity precisely as men do, or as the Spanish bulls, of which it is said that no more than one in twenty is fit to stand the combat of the arena. One grisly can scarcely be bullied into resistance; the next may fight to the end, against any odds, without flinching, or even attack unprovoked. Hence men of limited experience in this sport, generalizing from the actions of the two or three bears each has happened to see or kill, often reach diametrically opposite conclusions as to the fighting temper and capacity of the quarry. Even old hunters—who indeed, as a class, are very narrow-minded and opinionated—often generalize just as rashly as beginners. One will portray all bears as very dangerous; another will speak and act as if he deemed them of no more consequence than so many rabbits. I knew one old hunter who had killed a score without ever seeing one show fight. On the other hand, Dr. James C. Merrill, U.S.A., who has had about as much experience with bears as I have had, informs me that he has been charged with the utmost determination three times. In each case the attack was delivered before the bear was wounded or even shot at, the animal being roused by the approach of the hunters from his day bed, and charging headlong at them from a distance of twenty or thirty paces. All three bears were killed before they could do any damage. There was a very remarkable incident connected with the killing of one of them. It occurred in the northern spurs of the Bighorn range. Dr. Merrill, in company with an old hunter, had climbed down into a deep narrow canyon. The bottom was threaded with well-beaten elk trails. While following one of these the two men turned a corner of the canyon and were instantly charged by an old she-grisly, so close that it was only by good luck that one of the hurried shots disabled her and caused her to tumble over a cut bank where she was easily finished. They found that she had been lying directly across the game trail, on a smooth well beaten patch of bare earth, which looked as if it had been dug up, refilled, and trampled down.

Looking curiously at this patch they saw a bit of hide only partially covered at one end; digging down they found the body of a well grown grisly cub. Its skull had been crushed, and the brains licked out, and there were signs of other injuries. The hunters pondered long over this strange discovery, and hazarded many guesses as to its meaning. At last they decided that probably the cub had been killed, and its brains eaten out, either by some old male-grisly or by a cougar, that the mother had returned and driven away the murderer, and that she had then buried the body and lain above it, waiting to wreak her vengeance on the first passer-by.

Old Tazewell Woody, during his thirty years' life as a hunter in the Rockies and on the great plains, killed very many grislies. He always exercised much caution in dealing with them; and, as it happened, he was by some suitable tree in almost every case when he was charged. He would accordingly climb the tree (a practice of which I do not approve however); and the bear would look up at him and pass on without stopping. Once, when he was hunting in the mountains with a companion, the latter, who was down in a valley, while Woody was on the hillside, shot at a bear. The first thing Woody knew the wounded grisly, running up-hill, was almost on him from behind. As he turned it seized his rifle in its jaws. He wrenched the rifle round, while the bear still gripped it, and pulled trigger, sending a bullet into its shoulder; whereupon it struck him with its paw, and knocked him over the rocks. By good luck he fell in a snowbank and was not hurt in the least. Meanwhile the bear went on and they never got it.

Once he had an experience with a bear which showed a very curious mixture of rashness and cowardice. He and a companion were camped in a little tepee or wigwam, with a bright fire in front of it, lighting up the night. There was an inch of snow on the ground. Just after they went to bed a grisly came close to camp. Their dog rushed out and they could hear it bark round in the darkness for nearly an hour; then the bear drove it off and came right into camp. It went close to the fire, picking up the scraps of meat and bread, pulled a haunch of venison down from a tree, and passed and repassed in front of the tepee, paying no heed whatever to the two men, who crouched in the doorway talking to one another. Once it passed so close that Woody could almost have touched it. Finally his companion fired into it, and off it ran, badly wounded, without an attempt at retaliation. Next morning they followed its tracks in the snow, and found it a quarter of a mile away. It was near a pine and had buried itself under the loose earth, pine needles, and snow; Woody's companion almost walked over it, and putting his rifle to its ear blew out its brains.

In all his experience Woody had personally seen but four men who were badly mauled by bears. Three of these were merely wounded. One was bitten terribly in the back. Another had an arm partially chewed off. The third was a man named George Dow, and the accident happened to him on the Yellowstone, about the year 1878. He was with a pack animal at the time, leading it on a trail through a wood. Seeing a big she-bear with cubs he yelled at her; whereat she ran away, but only to cache her cubs, and in a minute, having hidden them, came racing back at him. His pack animal being slow he started to climb a tree; but before he could get far enough up she caught him, almost biting a piece out of the calf of his leg, pulled him down, bit and cuffed him two or three times, and then went on her way.

The only time Woody ever saw a man killed by a bear was once when he had given a touch of variety to his life by shipping on a New Bedford whaler which had touched at one of the Puget Sound ports. The whaler went up to a part of Alaska where bears were very plentiful and bold. One day a couple of boats' crews landed; and the men, who were armed only with an occasional harpoon or lance, scattered over the beach, one of them a Frenchman, wading into the water after shellfish. Suddenly a bear emerged from some bushes and charged among the astonished sailors, who scattered in every direction; but the bear, said Woody, "just had it in for that Frenchman," and went straight at him. Shrieking with terror he retreated up to his neck in the water, but the bear plunged in after him, caught him, and disembowelled him. One of the Yankee mates then fired a bomb lance into the bear's hips, and the savage beast hobbled off into the dense cover of the low scrub, where the enraged sailor folk were unable to get at it.

The truth is that while the grisly generally avoids a battle if possible, and often acts with great cowardice, it is never safe to take liberties with him; he usually fights desperately and dies hard when wounded and cornered, and exceptional individuals take the aggressive on small provocation.

During the years I lived on the frontier I came in contact with many persons who had been severely mauled or even crippled for life by grislies; and a number of cases where they killed men outright were also brought under my ken. Generally these accidents, as was natural, occurred to hunters who had roused or wounded the game.

A fighting bear sometimes uses his claws and sometimes his teeth. I have never known one to attempt to kill an antagonist by hugging, in spite of the popular belief to this effect; though he will sometimes draw an enemy towards him with his paws the better to reach him with his teeth, and to hold him so that he cannot escape from the biting. Nor does the bear often advance on his hind legs to the attack; though, if the man has come close to him in thick underbrush, or has stumbled on him in his lair unawares, he will often rise up in this fashion and strike a single blow. He will also rise in clinching with a man on horseback. In 1882 a mounted Indian was killed in this manner on one of the river bottoms some miles below where my ranch house now stands, not far from the function of the Beaver and Little Missouri. The bear had been hunted into a thicket by a band of Indians, in whose company my informant, a white squaw-man, with whom I afterward did some trading, was travelling. One of them in the excitement of the pursuit rode across the end of the thicket; as he did so the great beast sprang at him with wonderful quickness, rising on its hind legs, and knocking over the horse and rider with a single sweep of his terrible fore-paws. It then turned on the fallen man and tore him open, and though the other Indians came promptly to his rescue and slew his assailant, they were not in time to save their comrade's life.

A bear is apt to rely mainly on his teeth or claws according to whether his efforts are directed primarily to killing his foe or to making good his own escape. In the latter event he trusts chiefly to his claws. If cornered, he of course makes a rush for freedom, and in that case he downs any man who is in his way with a sweep of his great paw, but passes on without stopping to bite him. If while sleeping or resting in thick brush someone suddenly stumbles on him close up he pursues the same course, less from anger than from fear, being surprised and startled. Moreover, if attacked at close quarters by men and dogs he strikes right and left in defence.

Sometimes what is called a charge is rather an effort to get away. In localities where he has been hunted, a bear, like every other kind of game, is always on the look-out for an attack, and is prepared at any moment for immediate flight. He seems ever to have in his mind, whether feeding, sunning himself, or merely roaming around, the direction—usually towards the thickest cover or most broken ground—in which he intends to run if molested. When shot at he instantly starts towards this place; or he may be so confused that he simply runs he knows not whither; and in either event he may take a line that leads almost directly to or by the hunter, although he had at first no thought of charging. In such a case he usually strikes a single knock-down blow and gallops on without halting, though that one blow may have taken life. If the claws are long and fairly sharp (as in early spring, or even in the fall, if the animal has been working over soft ground) they add immensely to the effect of the blow, for they cut like blunt axes. Often, however, late in the season, and if the ground has been dry and hard, or rocky, the claws are worn down nearly to the quick, and the blow is then given mainly with the underside of the paw; although even under this disadvantage a thumb from a big bear will down a horse or smash in a man's breast. The hunter Hofer once lost a horse in this manner. He shot at and wounded a bear which rushed off, as ill luck would have it, past the place where his horse was picketed; probably more in fright than in anger it struck the poor beast a blow which, in the end, proved mortal.

If a bear means mischief and charges not to escape but to do damage, its aim is to grapple with or throw down its foe and bite him to death. The charge is made at a gallop, the animal sometimes coming on silently, with the mouth shut, and sometimes with the jaws open, the lips drawn back and teeth showing, uttering at the same time a succession of roars or of savage rasping snarls. Certain bears charge without any bluster and perfectly straight; while others first threaten and bully, and even when charging stop to growl, shake the head, and bite at a bush or knock holes in the ground with their fore-paws. Again, some of them charge home with a ferocious resolution which their extreme tenacity of life renders especially dangerous; while others can be turned or driven back even by a shot which is not mortal. They show the same variability in their behavior when wounded. Often a big bear, especially if charging, will receive a bullet in perfect silence, without flinching or seeming to pay any heed to it; while another will cry out and tumble about, and if charging, even though it may not abandon the attack, will pause for a moment to whine or bite at the wound.

Sometimes a single bite causes death. One of the most successful bear hunters I ever knew, an old fellow whose real name I never heard as he was always called Old Ike, was killed in this way in the spring or early summer of 1886 on one of the headwaters of the Salmon. He was a very good shot, had killed nearly a hundred bears with the rifle, and, although often charged, had never met with any accident, so that he had grown somewhat careless. On the day in question he had met a couple of mining prospectors and was travelling with them, when a grisly crossed his path. The old hunter immediately ran after it, rapidly gaining, as the bear did not hurry when it saw itself pursued, but slouched slowly forwards, occasionally turning its head to grin and growl. It soon went into a dense grove of young spruce, and as the hunter reached the edge it charged fiercely out. He fired one hasty shot, evidently wounding the animal, but not seriously enough to stop or cripple it; and as his two companions ran forward they saw the bear seize him with is widespread jaws, forcing him to the ground. They shouted and fired, and the beast abandoned the fallen man on the instant and sullenly retreated into the spruce thicket, whither they dared not follow it. Their friend was at his last gasp; for the whole side of the chest had been crushed in by the one bite, the lungs showing between the rent ribs.

Very often, however, a bear does not kill a man by one bite, but after throwing him lies on him, biting him to death. Usually, if no assistance is at hand, such a man is doomed; although if he pretends to be dead, and has the nerve to lie quiet under very rough treatment, it is just possible that the bear may leave him alive, perhaps after half burying what it believes to be the body. In a very few exceptional instances men of extraordinary prowess with the knife have succeeded in beating off a bear, and even in mortally wounding it, but in most cases a single-handed struggle, at close quarters, with a grisly bent on mischief, means death.

Occasionally the bear, although vicious, is also frightened, and passes on after giving one or two bites; and frequently a man who is knocked down is rescued by his friends before he is killed, the big beast mayhap using his weapons with clumsiness. So a bear may kill a foe with a single blow of its mighty fore-arm, either crushing in the head or chest by sheer force of sinew, or else tearing open the body with its formidable claws; and so on the other hand he may, and often does, merely disfigure or maim the foe by a hurried stroke. Hence it is common to see men who have escaped the clutches of a grisly, but only at the cost of features marred beyond recognition, or a body rendered almost helpless for life. Almost every old resident of western Montana or northern Idaho has known two or three unfortunates who have suffered in this manner. I have myself met one such man in Helena, and another in Missoula; both were living at least as late as 1889, the date at which I last saw them. One had been partially scalped by a bear's teeth; the animal was very old and so the fangs did not enter the skull. The other had been bitten across the face, and the wounds never entirely healed, so that his disfigured visage was hideous to behold.

Most of these accidents occur in following a wounded or worried bear into thick cover; and under such circumstances an animal apparently hopelessly disabled, or in the death throes, may with a last effort kill one or more of its assailants. In 1874 my wife's uncle, Captain Alexander Moore, U.S.A., and my friend Captain Bates, with some men of the 2d and 3d Cavalry, were scouting in Wyoming, near the Freezeout Mountains. One morning they roused a bear in the open prairie and followed it at full speed as it ran towards a small creek. At one spot in the creek beavers had built a dam, and as usual in such places there was a thick growth of bushes and willow saplings. Just as the bear reached the edge of this little jungle it was struck by several balls, both of its forelegs being broken. Nevertheless, it managed to shove itself forward on its hind-legs, and partly rolled, partly pushed itself into the thicket, the bushes though low being so dense that its body was at once completely hidden. The thicket was a mere patch of brush, not twenty yards across in any direction. The leading troopers reached the edge almost as the bear tumbled in. One of them, a tall and powerful man named Miller, instantly dismounted and prepared to force his way in among the dwarfed willows, which were but breast high. Among the men who had ridden up were Moore and Bates, and also the two famous scouts, Buffalo Bill—long a companion of Captain Moore—and California Joe, Custer's faithful follower. California Joe had spent almost all his life on the plains and in the mountains, as a hunter and Indian fighter; and when he saw the trooper about to rush into the thicket he called out to him not to do so, warning him of the danger. But the man was a very reckless fellow and he answered by jeering at the old hunter for his over-caution in being afraid of a crippled bear. California Joe made no further effort to dissuade him, remarking quietly: "Very well, sonny, go in; it's your own affair." Miller then leaped off the bank on which they stood and strode into the thicket, holding his rifle at the port. Hardly had he taken three steps when the bear rose in front of him, roaring with rage and pain. It was so close that the man had no chance to fire. Its fore-arms hung useless and as it reared unsteadily on its hind-legs, lunging forward at him, he seized it by the ears and strove to hold it back. His strength was very great, and he actually kept the huge head from his face and braced himself so that he was not overthrown; but the bear twisted its muzzle from side to side, biting and tearing the man's arms and shoulders. Another soldier jumping down slew the beast with a single bullet, and rescued his comrade; but though alive he was too badly hurt to recover and died after reaching the hospital. Buffalo Bill was given the bearskin, and I believe has it now.

The instances in which hunters who have rashly followed grislies into thick cover have been killed or severely mauled might be multiplied indefinitely. I have myself known of eight cases in which men have met their deaths in this manner.

It occasionally happens that a cunning old grisly will lie so close that the hunter almost steps on him; and he then rises suddenly with a loud, coughing growl and strikes down or seizes the man before the latter can fire off his rifle. More rarely a bear which is both vicious and crafty deliberately permits the hunter to approach fairly near to, or perhaps pass by, its hiding-place, and then suddenly charges him with such rapidity that he has barely time for the most hurried shot. The danger in such a case is of course great.

Ordinarily, however, even in the brush, the bear's object is to slink away, not to fight, and very many are killed even under the most unfavorable circumstances without accident. If an unwounded bear thinks itself unobserved it is not apt to attack; and in thick cover it is really astonishing to see how one of these large animals can hide, and how closely it will lie when there is danger. About twelve miles below my ranch there are some large river bottoms and creek bottoms covered with a matted mass of cottonwood, box-alders, bullberry bushes, rose-bushes, ash, wild plums, and other bushes. These bottoms have harbored bears ever since I first saw them; but though, often in company with a large party, I have repeatedly beaten through them, and though we must at times have been very near indeed to the game, we never so much as heard it run.

When bears are shot, as they usually must be, in open timber or on the bare mountain, the risk is very much less. Hundreds may thus be killed with comparatively little danger; yet even under these circumstances they will often charge, and sometimes make their charge good. The spice of danger, especially to a man armed with a good repeating rifle, is only enough to add zest to the chase, and the chief triumph is in outwitting the wary quarry and getting within range. Ordinarily the only excitement is in the stalk, the bear doing nothing more than keep a keen lookout and manifest the utmost anxiety to get away. As is but natural, accidents occasionally occur; yet they are usually due more to some failure in man or weapon than to the prowess of the bear. A good hunter whom I once knew, at a time when he was living in Butte, received fatal injuries from a bear he attacked in open woodland. The beast charged after the first shot, but slackened its pace on coming almost up to the man. The latter's gun jammed, and as he was endeavoring to work it he kept stepping slowly back, facing the bear which followed a few yards distant, snarling and threatening. Unfortunately, while thus walking backwards, the man struck a dead log and fell over it, whereupon the beast instantly sprang on him and mortally wounded him before help arrived.

On rare occasions men who are not at the time hunting it fall victims to the grisly. This is usually because they stumble on it unawares and the animal attacks them more in fear than in anger. One such case, resulting fatally, occurred near my own ranch. The man walked almost over a bear while crossing a little point of brush, in a bend of the river, and was brained with a single blow of the paw. In another instance which came to my knowledge the man escaped with a shaking up, and without even a fright. His name was Perkins, and he was out gathering huckleberries in the woods on a mountain side near Pend Oreille Lake. Suddenly he was sent flying head over heels, by a blow which completely knocked the breath out of his body; and so instantaneous was the whole affair that all he could ever recollect about it was getting a vague glimpse of the bear just as he was bowled over. When he came to he found himself lying some distance down the hill-side, much shaken, and without his berry pail, which had rolled a hundred yards below him, but not otherwise the worse for his misadventure; while the footprints showed that the bear, after delivering the single hurried stroke at the unwitting disturber of its day-dreams, had run off up-hill as fast as it was able.

A she-bear with cubs is a proverbially dangerous beast; yet even under such conditions different grislies act in directly opposite ways. Some she-grislies, when their cubs are young, but are able to follow them about, seem always worked up to the highest pitch of anxious and jealous rage, so that they are likely to attack unprovoked any intruder or even passer-by. Others when threatened by the hunter leave their cubs to their fate without a visible qualm of any kind, and seem to think only of their own safety.

In 1882 Mr. Caspar W. Whitney, now of New York, met with a very singular adventure with a she-bear and cub. He was in Harvard when I was, but left it and, like a good many other Harvard men of that time, took to cow-punching in the West. He went on a ranch in Rio Arriba County, New Mexico, and was a keen hunter, especially fond of the chase of cougar, bear, and elk. One day while riding a stony mountain trail he saw a little grisly cub watching him from the chaparral above, and he dismounted to try to capture it; his rifle was a 40–90 Sharp's. Just as he neared the cub, he heard a growl and caught a glimpse of the old she, and he at once turned up-hill, and stood under some tall, quaking aspens. From this spot he fired at and wounded the she, then seventy yards off; and she charged furiously. He hit her again, but as she kept coming like a thunderbolt he climbed hastily up the aspen, dragging his gun with him, as it had a strap. When the bear reached the foot of the aspen she reared, and bit and clawed the slender trunk, shaking it for moment, and he shot her through the eye. Off she sprang for a few yards, and then spun round a dozen times, as if dazed or partially stunned; for the bullet had not touched the brain. Then the vindictive and resolute beast came back to the tree and again reared up against it; this time to receive a bullet that dropped her lifeless. Mr. Whitney then climbed down and walked to where the cub had been sitting as a looker-on. The little animal did not move until he reached out his hand; when it suddenly struck at him like an angry cat, dove into the bushes, and was seen no more.

In the summer of 1888 an old-time trapper, named Charley Norton, while on Loon Creek, of the middle fork of the Salmon, meddled with a she and her cubs. She ran at him and with one blow of her paw almost knocked off his lower jaw; yet he recovered, and was alive when I last heard of him.

Yet the very next spring the cowboys with my own wagon on the Little Missouri round-up killed a mother bear which made but little more fight than a coyote. She had two cubs, and was surprised in the early morning on the prairie far from cover. There were eight or ten cowboys together at the time, just starting off on a long circle, and of course they all got down their ropes in a second, and putting spurs to their fiery little horses started toward the bears at a run, shouting and swinging their loops round their heads. For a moment the old she tried to bluster and made a half-hearted threat of charging; but her courage failed before the rapid onslaught of her yelling, rope-swinging assailants; and she took to her heels and galloped off, leaving the cubs to shift for themselves. The cowboys were close behind, however, and after a half a mile's run she bolted into a shallow cave or hole in the side of a butte, where she stayed cowering and growling, until one of the men leaped off his horse, ran up to the edge of the hole, and killed her with a single bullet from his revolver, fired so close that the powder burned her hair. The unfortunate cubs were roped, and then so dragged about that they were speedily killed instead of being brought alive to camp, as ought to have been done.

In the cases mentioned above the grisly attacked only after having been itself assailed, or because it feared an assault, for itself or for its young. In the old days, however, it may almost be said that a grisly was more apt to attack than to flee. Lewis and Clarke and the early explorers who immediately succeeded them, as well as the first hunters and trappers, the "Rocky Mountain Men" of the early decades of the present century, were repeatedly assailed in this manner; and not a few of the bear hunters of that period found that it was unnecessary to take much trouble about approaching their quarry, as the grisly was usually prompt to accept the challenge and to advance of its own accord, as soon as it discovered the foe. All this is changed now. Yet even at the present day an occasional vicious old bear may be found, in some far off and little trod fastness, which still keeps up the former habit of its kind. All old hunters have tales of this sort to relate, the prowess, cunning, strength, and ferocity of the grisly being favorite topics for campfire talk throughout the Rockies; but in most cases it is not safe to accept these stories without careful sifting.

Still, it is just as unsafe to reject them all. One of my own cowboys was once attacked by a grisly, seemingly in pure wantonness. He was riding up a creek bottom, and had just passed a clump of rose and bullberry bushes when his horse gave such a leap as almost to unseat him, and then darted madly forward. Turning round in the saddle to his utter astonishment he saw a large bear galloping after him, at the horse's heels. For a few jumps the race was close, then the horse drew away and the bear wheeled and went into a thicket of wild plums. The amazed and indignant cowboy, as soon as he could rein in his steed, drew his revolver and rode back to and around the thicket, endeavoring to provoke his late pursuer to come out and try conclusions on more equal terms; but prudent Ephraim had apparently repented of his freak of ferocious bravado, and declined to leave the secure shelter of the jungle.

Other attacks are of a much more explicable nature. Mr. Huffman, the photographer, of Miles City, informed me that once when butchering some slaughtered elk he was charged twice by a she-bear and two well-grown cubs. This was a piece of sheer bullying, undertaken solely with the purpose of driving away the man and feasting on the carcasses; for in each charge the three bears, after advancing with much bluster, roaring, and growling, halted just before coming to close quarters. In another instance a gentleman I once knew, a Mr. S. Carr, was charged by a grisly from mere ill temper at being disturbed at mealtime. The man was riding up a valley; and the bear was at an elk carcass, near a clump of firs. As soon as it became aware of the approach of the horseman, while he was yet over a hundred yards distant, it jumped on the carcass, looked at him a moment, and then ran straight for him. There was no particular reason why it should have charged, for it was fat and in good trim, though when killed its head showed scars made by the teeth of rival grislies. Apparently it had been living so well, principally on flesh, that it had become quarrelsome; and perhaps its not over sweet disposition had been soured by combats with others of its own kind. In yet another case, a grisly charged with even less excuse. An old trapper, from whom I occasionally bought fur, was toiling up a mountain pass when he spied a big bear sitting on his haunches on the hillside above. The trapper shouted and waved his cap; whereupon, to his amazement, the bear uttered a loud "wough" and charged straight down on him—only to fall a victim to misplaced boldness.

I am even inclined to think that there have been wholly exceptional occasions when a grisly has attacked a man with the deliberate purpose of making a meal of him; when, in other words, it has started on the career of a man-eater. At least, on any other theory I find it difficult to account for an attack which once came to my knowledge. I was at Sand Point, on Pend'Oreille Lake, and met some French and Méti trappers, then in town with their bales of beaver, otter, and sable. One of them, who gave his name as Baptiste Lamoche, had his head twisted over to one side, the result of the bite of a bear. When the accident occurred he was out on a trapping trip with two companions. They had pitched camp right on the shore of a cove in a little lake, and his comrades were off fishing in a dugout or pirogue. He himself was sitting near the shore, by a little lean-to, watching some beaver meat which was sizzling over the dying embers. Suddenly, and without warning, a great bear, which had crept silently up beneath the shadows of the tall evergreens, rushed at him, with a guttural roar, and seized him before he could rise to his feet. It grasped him with its jaws at the junction of the neck and shoulder, making the teeth meet through bone, sinew, and muscle; and turning, racked off towards the forest, dragging with it the helpless and paralyzed victim. Luckily the two men in the canoe had just paddled round the point, in sight of, and close to, camp. The man in the bow, seeing the plight of their comrade, seized his rifle and fired at the bear. The bullet went through the beast's lungs, and it forthwith dropped its prey, and running off some two hundred yards, lay down on its side and died. The rescued man recovered full health and strength, but never again carried his head straight.

Old hunters and mountain-men tell many stories, not only of malicious grislies thus attacking men in camp, but also of their even dogging the footsteps of some solitary hunter and killing him when the favorable opportunity occurs. Most of these tales are mere fables; but it is possible that in altogether exceptional instances they rest on a foundation of fact. One old hunter whom I knew told me such a story. He was a truthful old fellow, and there was no doubt that he believed what he said, and that his companion was actually killed by a bear; but it is probable that he was mistaken in reading the signs of his comrade's fate, and that the latter was not dogged by the bear at all, but stumbled on him and was slain in the surprise of the moment.

At any rate, cases of wanton assaults by grislies are altogether out of the common. The ordinary hunter may live out his whole life in the wilderness and never know aught of a bear attacking a man unprovoked; and the great majority of bears are shot under circumstances of no special excitement, as they either make no fight at all, or, if they do fight, are killed before there is any risk of their doing damage. If surprised on the plains, at some distance from timber or from badly broken ground, it is no uncommon feat for a single horseman to kill them with a revolver. Twice of late years it has been performed in the neighborhood of my ranch. In both instances the men were not hunters out after game, but simply cowboys, riding over the range in the early morning in pursuance of their ordinary duties among the cattle. I knew both men and have worked with them on the round-up. Like most cowboys they carried 44-calibre Colt revolvers, and were accustomed to and fairly expert in their use, and they were mounted on ordinary cow-ponies—quick, wiry, plucky little beasts. In one case the bear was seen from quite a distance, lounging across a broad tableland. The cowboy, by taking advantage of a winding and rather shallow coulie, got quite close to him. He then scrambled out of the coulie, put spurs to his pony, and raced up to within fifty yards of the astonished bear ere the latter quite understood what it was that was running at him through the gray dawn. He made no attempt at fight, but ran at top speed towards a clump of brush not far off at the head of a creek. Before he could reach it, however, the galloping horseman was alongside, and fired three shots into his broad back. He did not turn, but ran on into the bushes and then fell over and died.

In the other case the cowboy, a Texan, was mounted on a good cutting pony, a spirited, handy, agile little animal, but excitable, and with a habit of dancing, which rendered it difficult to shoot from its back. The man was with the round-up wagon, and had been sent off by himself to make a circle through some low, barren buttes, where it was not thought more than a few head of stock would be found. On rounding the corner of a small washout he almost ran over a bear which was feeding on the carcass of a steer that had died in an alkali hole. After a moment of stunned surprise the bear hurled himself at the intruder with furious impetuosity; while the cowboy, wheeling his horse on its haunches and dashing in the spurs, carried it just clear of his assailant's headlong rush. After a few springs he reined in and once more wheeled half round, having drawn his revolver, only to find the bear again charging and almost on him. This time he fired into it, near the joining of the neck and shoulder, the bullet going downwards into the chest hollow; and again by a quick dash to one side he just avoided the rush of the beast and the sweep of its mighty fore-paw. The beast then halted for a minute, and he rode close by it at a run, firing a couple of shots, which brought on another resolute charge. The ground was somewhat rugged and broken, but his pony was as quick on its feet as a cat, and never stumbled, even when going at full speed to avoid the bear's first mad rushes. It speedily became so excited, however, as to render it almost impossible for the rider to take aim. Sometimes he would come up close to the bear and wait for it to charge, which it would do, first at a trot, or rather rack, and then at a lumbering but swift gallop; and he would fire one or two shots before being forced to run. At other times, if the bear stood still in a good place, he would run by it, firing as he rode. He spent many cartridges, and though most of them were wasted, occasionally a bullet went home. The bear fought with the most savage courage, champing its bloody jaws, roaring with rage, and looking the very incarnation of evil fury. For some minutes it made no effort to flee, either charging or standing at bay. Then it began to move slowly towards a patch of ash and wild plums in the head of a coulie, some distance off. Its pursuer rode after it, and when close enough would push by it and fire, while the bear would spin quickly round and charge as fiercely as ever, though evidently beginning to grow weak. At last, when still a couple of hundred yards from cover the man found he had used up all his cartridges, and then merely followed at a safe distance. The bear no longer paid heed to him, but walked slowly forwards, swaying its great head from side to side, while the blood streamed from between its half-opened jaws. On reaching the cover he could tell by the waving of the bushes that it walked to the middle and then halted. A few minutes afterwards some of the other cowboys rode up, having been attracted by the incessant firing. They surrounded the thicket, firing and throwing stones into the bushes. Finally, as nothing moved, they ventured in and found the indomitable grisly warrior lying dead.

Cowboys delight in nothing so much as the chance to show their skill as riders and ropers; and they always try to ride down and rope any wild animal they come across in favorable ground and close enough up. If a party of them meets a bear in the open they have great fun; and the struggle between the shouting, galloping rough-riders and their shaggy quarry is full of wild excitement and not unaccompanied by danger. The bear often throws the noose from his head so rapidly that it is a difficult matter to catch him; and his frequent charges scatter his tormentors in every direction while the horses become wild with fright over the roaring, bristling beast—for horses seem to dread a bear more than any other animal. If the bear cannot reach cover, however, his fate is sealed. Sooner or later, the noose tights over one leg, or perchance over the neck and fore-paw, and as the rope straightens with a "pluck," the horse braces itself desperately and the bear tumbles over. Whether he regains his feet or not the cowboy keeps the rope taut; soon another noose tightens over a leg, and the bear is speedily rendered helpless.

I have known of these feats being performed several times in northern Wyoming, although never in the immediate neighborhood of my ranch. Mr. Archibald Rogers' cowhands have in this manner caught several bears, on or near his ranch on the Gray Bull, which flows into the Bighorn; and those of Mr. G. B. Grinnell

have also occasionally done so. Any set of moderately good ropers
and riders, who are accustomed to back one another up and act
together, can accomplish the feat if they have smooth ground and
plenty of room. It is, however, indeed a feat of skill and daring for
a single man; and yet I have known of more than one instance in
which it has been accomplished by some reckless knight of the rope
and the saddle. One such occurred in 1887 on the Flathead Reservation, the hero being a half-breed; and another in 1890 at the
mouth of the Bighorn, where a cowboy roped, bound, and killed a
large bear single-handed.

My friend General "Red" Jackson, of Bellemeade, in the pleasant mid-county of Tennessee, once did a feat which casts into the
shade even the feats of the men of the lariat. General Jackson, who
afterwards became one of the ablest and most renowned of the
Confederate cavalry leaders, was at the time a young officer in the
Mounted Rifle Regiment, now known as the 3d University States
Cavalry. It was some years before the Civil War, and the regiment
was on duty in the southwest, then the debatable land of Coman-
che and Apache. While on a scout after hostile Indians, the troops
in their march roused a large grisly which sped off across the plain
in front of them. Strict orders had been issued against firing at
game, because of the nearness of the Indians. Young Jackson was a
man of great strength, a keen swordsman, who always kept the finest edge on his blade, and he was on a swift and mettled Kentucky
horse, which luckily had but one eye. Riding at full speed he soon
overtook the quarry. As the horse hoofs sounded nearer, the grim
bear ceased its flight, and whirling round stood at bay, raising itself
on its hind-legs and threatening its pursuer with bared fangs and
spread claws. Carefully riding his horse so that its blind side should

be towards the monster, the cavalryman swept by at a run, handling his steed with such daring skill that he just cleared the blow of the dreaded fore-paw, while with one mighty sabre stroke he cleft the bear's skull, slaying the grinning beast as it stood upright.

CHAPTER EIGHT

The Black Bear

Theodore Roosevelt

———

(Excerpted from The Wilderness Hunter.*)*

MANY OF THE TWENTY-SIXTH PRESIDENT'S BOOKS WERE AS IMPORTANT A part of his hunting kit as were his guns and loads, and he turned their pages by flickering firelight in places ranging from his ranch house to campfires on the prairie to tent camps on the African veldt. TR touches on his passion for reading being intertwined with his love of the outdoors in his autobiography (Theodore Roosevelt: An Autobiography, *1913*):

> *There are men who love out-of-doors who yet never open a book, and other men who love books but to whom the great book of nature is a sealed volume, and the lines written therein blurred and illegible. Nevertheless among those men whom I have known the love of books and the love of outdoors, in their highest expressions, have usually gone hand in hand. . . . Usually the keenest appreciation of what is seen in nature is to be found of those who have also profited by the hoarded and recorded wisdom of their fellow men?*

Roosevelt gave us a good look at his grizzly bear experiences in an earlier chapter. Now he turns his attention to the black bear—not as exciting as the grizzly, but always interesting.

Next to the whitetail deer the black bear is the commonest and most widely distributed of American big game. It is still found quite plentifully in northern New England, in the Adirondacks, Catskills, and along the entire length of the Alleghenies, as well as in the swamps and canebrakes of the southern States. It is also common in the great forests of northern Michigan, Wisconsin, and Minnesota, and throughout the Rocky Mountains and the timbered ranges of the Pacific coast. In the East it has always ranked second only to the deer among the beasts of chase. The bear and the buck were the staple objects of pursuit of all the old hunters. They were more plentiful than the bison and elk even in the long vanished days when these two great monarchs of the forest still ranged eastward to Virginia and Pennsylvania. The wolf and the cougar were always too scarce and too shy to yield much profit to the hunter. The black bear is a timid, cowardly animal, and usually a vegetarian, though it sometimes preys on the sheep, hogs, and even cattle of the settler, and is very fond of raiding his corn and melons. Its meat is good and its fur often valuable, and in its chase there is much excitement, and occasionally a slight spice of danger, just enough to render it attractive; so it has always been eagerly followed. Yet it still holds it own, though in greatly diminished numbers, in the more thinly settled portions of the country. One of the standing riddles of American zoölogy is the fact that the black bear, which is easier killed and less prolific than the wolf, should hold its own in the land better than the latter, this being directly the reverse of what occurs in Europe, where the brown bear is generally exterminated before the wolf.

In a few wild spots in the East, in northern Maine for instance, here and there in the neighborhood of the upper Great Lakes, in the east Tennessee and Kentucky mountains and the swamps of Florida and Mississippi, there still lingers an occasional representative of the old wilderness hunters. These men live in log-cabins in the wilderness. They do their hunting on foot, occasionally with the help of a single trailing dog. In Maine they are as apt to kill moose and caribou as bear and deer; but elsewhere the two last, with an occasional cougar or wolf, are the beasts of chase which they follow. Nowadays as these old hunters die there is no one to take their places, though there are still plenty of backwoods settlers in all of the regions named who do a great deal of hunting and trapping. Such an old hunter rarely makes his appearance at the settlements except to dispose of his peltry and hides in exchange for cartridges and provisions, and he leads a life of such lonely isolation as to insure his individual characteristics developing into peculiarities. Most of the wilder districts in the eastern States still preserve memories of some such old hunter who lived his long life alone, waging ceaseless warfare on the vanishing game, whose oddities, as well as his courage, hardihood, and woodcraft, are laughingly remembered by the older settlers, and who is usually best known as having killed the last wolf or bear or cougar ever seen in the locality.

Generally the weapon mainly relied on by these old hunters is the rifle; and occasionally some old hunter will be found even to this day who uses a muzzle loader, such as Kit Carson carried in the middle of the century. There are exceptions to this rule of the rifle however. In the years after the Civil War one of the many noted hunters of southwest Virginia and east Tennessee was Wilbur Waters, sometimes called The Hunter of White Top. He often killed black bear with a knife and dogs. He spent all his life in hunting and was very successful, killing the last gang of wolves to be found in his neighborhood; and he slew innumerable bears, with no worse results to himself than an occasional bite or scratch.

In the southern States the planters living in the wilder regions have always been in the habit of following the black bear with horse and hound, many of them keeping regular packs of bear hounds. Such a pack includes not only pure-bred hounds, but also cross-bred animals, and some sharp, agile, hard-biting fierce dogs and terriers. They follow the bear and bring him to bay but do not try to kill him, although there are dogs of the big fighting breeds which can readily master a black bear if loosed at him three or four at a time; but the dogs of these southern bear-hound packs are not fitted for such work, and if they try to close with the bear he is certain to play havoc with them, disembowelling them with blows of his paws or seizing them in his arms and biting through their spines or legs. The riders follow the hounds through the cane-brakes, and also try to make cutoffs and station themselves at open points where they think the bear will pass, so that they may get a shot at him. The weapons used are rifles, shotguns, and occasionally revolvers.

Sometimes, however, the hunter uses the knife. General Wade Hampton, who has probably killed more black bears than any other man living in the United States, frequently used the knife, slaying thirty or forty with his weapon. His plan was, when he found that the dogs had the bear at bay, to walk up close and cheer them on. They would instantly seize the bear in a body, and he would then rush in and stab it behind the shoulder, reaching over so as to inflict the wound on the opposite side from that where he stood. He escaped scathless from all these encounters save one, in which he was rather severely torn in the forearm. Many other hunters have used the knife, but perhaps none so frequently as he; for he was always fond of steel, as witness his feats with the "white arm" during the Civil War.

General Hampton always hunted with large packs of hounds, managed sometimes by himself and sometimes by his negro hunt-ers. He occasionally took out forty dogs at a time. He found that all his dogs together could not kill a big fat bear, but they occa-sionally killed three-year-olds, or lean and poor bears. During the course of his life he has himself killed, or been in at the death of, five hundred bears, at least two thirds of them falling by his own hand. In the years just before the war he had on one occasion, in Mississippi, killed sixty-eight bears in five months. Once he killed four bears in a day; at another time three, and frequently two. The two largest bears he himself killed weighed, respectively, 408 and 410 pounds. They were both shot in Mississippi. But he saw at least one bear killed which was much larger than either of these. These figures were taken down at the time, when the animals were actually weighed on the scales. Most of his hunting for bear was done in northern Mississippi, where one of his plantations was situated, near Greenville. During the half century that he hunted, on and off, in this neighborhood, he knew of two instances where hunters were fatally wounded in the chase of the black bear. Both of the men were inexperienced, one being a raftsman who came down the river, and the other a man from Vicksburg. He was not able to learn the particulars in the last case, but the raftsman came too close to a bear that was at bay, and it broke through the dogs, rushed at and overthrew him, then lying on him, it bit him deeply in the thigh, through the femoral artery, so that he speedily bled to death.

But a black bear is not usually a formidable opponent, and though he will sometimes charge home he is much more apt to bluster and bully than actually to come to close quarters. I myself have but once seen a man who had been hurt by one of these bears. This was an Indian. He had come on the beast close up in a thick wood, and had mortally wounded it with his gun; it had then closed with him, knocking the gun out of his hand, so that he was forced to use his knife. It charged him on all fours, but in the grapple, when it had failed to throw him down, it raised itself on its hind legs, clasping him across the shoulders with its fore-paws. Apparently it had no intention of hugging, but merely sought to draw him within reach of his jaws. He fought desperately against this, using the knife freely, and striving to keep its head back; and the flow of blood weakened the animal, so that it finally fell exhausted, before being able dangerously to injure him. But it had bitten his left arm very severely, and its claws had made long gashes on his shoulders.

Black bears, like grislies, vary greatly in their modes of attack. Sometimes they rush in and bite; and again they strike with their fore-paws. Two of my cowboys were originally from Maine, where I knew them well. There they were fond of trapping bears, and caught a good many. The huge steel gins, attached by chains to heavy clogs, prevented the trapped beasts from gong far, and when found they were always tied tight round some tree or bush, and usually nearly exhausted. The men killed them either with a little 32-calibre pistol or a hatchet. But once did they meet with any difficulty. On this occasion one of them incautiously approached a captured bear to knock it on the head with his hatchet, but the animal managed to partially untwist itself, and with its free forearm made a rapid sweep at him; he jumped back just in time, the bear's claws tearing his clothes—after which he shot it. Bears are shy and have very keen noses; they are therefore hard to kill by fair hunting, living, as they generally do, in dense forests or thick brush. They are easy enough to trap, however. Thus, these two men, though they trapped so many, never but once killed them in any other way. On this occasion one of them, in the winter, found in a great hollow log a den where a she and two well-grown cubs had taken up their abode, and shot all three with his rifle as they burst out.

Where they are much hunted, bear become purely nocturnal; but in the wilder forests I have seen them abroad at all hours, though they do not much relish the intense heat of noon. They are rather comical animals to watch feeding and going about the ordinary business of their lives. Once I spent half an hour lying at the edge of a wood and looking at a black bear some three hundred yards off across an open glade. It was in good stalking country, but the wind was unfavorable and I waited for it to shift—waited too long as it proved, for something frightened the beast and he made off before I could get a shot at him. When I first saw him he was shuffling along and rooting in the ground, so that he looked like a great pig. Then he began to turn over the stones and logs to hunt for insects, small reptiles, and the like. A moderate-sized stone he would turn over with a single clap of his paw, and then plunge his nose down into the hollow to gobble up the small creatures beneath while still dazed by the light. The big logs and rocks he would tug and worry at with both paws; once, over-exerting his clumsy strength, he lost his grip and rolled clean on his back. Under some of the logs he evidently found mice and chipmunks; then, as soon as the log was overturned, he would be seen jumping about with grotesque agility, and making quick dabs here and there, as the little scurrying rodent turned and twisted, until at last he put his paw on it and scooped it up into his mouth. Sometimes, probably when he smelt the mice underneath, he would cautiously turn the log over with one paw, holding the other lifted and ready to strike. Now and then he would halt and sniff the air in every direction, and it was after one of these halts that he suddenly shuffled off into the woods.

Black bear generally feed on berries, nuts, insects, carrion, and the like; but at times they take to killing very large animals. In fact, they are curiously irregular in their food. They will kill deer if they can get at them; but generally the deer are too quick. Sheep and hogs are their favorite prey, especially the latter, for bears seem to have a special relish for pork. Twice I have known a black bear kill cattle. Once the victim was a bull which had got mired, and which the bear deliberately proceeded to eat alive, heedless of the bellows of the unfortunate beast. On the other occasion, a cow was surprised and slain among some bushes at the edge of a remote pasture. In the spring, soon after the long winter sleep, they are very hungry, and are especially apt to attack large beasts at this time; although during the very first days of their appearance, when they are just breaking their fast, they eat rather sparingly, and by preference the tender shoots of green grass and other herbs, or frogs and crayfish; it is not for a week or two that they seem to be overcome by lean, ravenous hunger. They will even attack and master that formidable fighter the moose, springing at it from an ambush as it passes— for a bull moose would surely be an overmatch for one of them if fronted fairly in the open. An old hunter, whom I could trust, told me that he had seen in the snow in early spring the place where a bear had sprung at two moose, which were trotting together; he missed his spring, and the moose got off, their strides after they settled down into their pace being tremendous, and showing how thoroughly they were frightened. Another time he saw a bear chase a moose into a lake, where it waded out a little distance, and then turned to bay, bidding defiance to his pursuer, the latter not daring to approach in the water. I have been told—but cannot vouch for it—that instances have been known where the bear, maddened by hunger, has gone in on a moose thus standing at bay, only to be beaten down under the water by the terrible fore-hoofs of the quarry, and to yield its life in the contest. A lumberman told me that he once saw a moose, evidently much startled, trot through a swamp, and immediately afterwards a bear came up following the tracks. He almost ran into the man, and was evidently not in a good temper, for he growled and blustered, and two or three times made feints of charging, before he finally concluded to go off.

Bears will occasionally visit hunters' or lumbermen's camps, in the absence of the owners, and play sad havoc with all there therein is, devouring everything eatable, especially if sweet, and trampling into a dirty mess whatever they do not eat. The black bear does not average more than a third the size of the grisly; but, like all its kind, it varies greatly in weight. The largest I myself ever saw weighed was in Maine, and tipped the scale at 346 pounds; but I have a perfectly authentic record of one in Maine that weighed 397, and my friend, Dr. Hart Merriam, tells me that he has seen several in the Adirondacks that when killed weighed about 350.

I myself shot but one or two black bears, and these were obtained under circumstances of no special interest, as I merely stumbled on them while after other game, and killed them before they had a chance either to run or show fight.

CHAPTER NINE

The Alaskan Grizzly

Harold McCracken

(Excerpted from "The Alaskan Grizzly.")

DEPENDING ON THEIR HOME GROUNDS—RANGING FROM RIVERS PACKED with salmon to mountain forests where caribou dwell—these bears range in size from normal to super-giant-sized. When their paths cross with humans, anything can happen.

The great Alaskan grizzly—the Kodiak brown bear (*Ursus middendorffi*) and its even larger Alaska Peninsula brother (*Ursus gyas*)—is probably as far famed as either the African lion or the Bengal tiger. And yet, probably less is known of its life history than of any of the other larger mammals. He is, nevertheless, a sort of fictitious by-word at the hearths of all those hunter-sportsmen who enjoy the savor of genuine hazard in their quest for sport and trophies. A beast whom most prefer to "talk" about hunting, rather than face in mortal combat. And his 1,000 to 2,000 pounds of brawn and power is unquestionably the embodiment of all that even the most adventurous care to seek. He is supreme in size, in brute power, as well as in physical dexterity, sagacity, and pernicious damnableness in the animal kingdom. And this, not in the mere belief of a casual observer, but weighed and tried on the scales of science. To go into details regarding the life history, the "whys" and "whens" and "hows" of his life career, would entail a goodly volume, which, though immensely interesting in every detail, would be far too cumbersome in such a place as this.

His home is that long, slightly curved arm that reaches out from the southwestern corner of Alaska, separating the North Pacific Ocean from the Bering Sea, and dabbling off in the spattered Aleutian Islands. The Alaska Peninsula is today one of the most wild, least visited and less known of all the districts on this continent.

But in reality, the Alaska Peninsula is, for the most part, a terribly wild Garden of Eden. Its waterways boast more fine fish than any other similar sized section of the globe; on its rounded undulating hills and tundra lands are great herds of caribou, the finest of edible flesh; it is carpeted with berry bushes; there are fine furred animals in abundance; millions of wildfowl, duck, geese, eiders, seals, sea lions; big bears—everything necessary for the welfare and happiness of primitive man. It is a truly primitive land.

While the great Alaska Peninsula bear is a carnivore, or flesh eater—and what applies to this bear also applies in many respects to his brothers, the sub- and sub-sub-species of other districts of Alaska—yet he has frequently and correctly been called "the great grass-eating bear" and also "the great fish-eating bear." All animals subsist in the manner and on the foods that demand the least efforts, hazard and inconvenience to their life and comforts. Thus the bears of the Alaska Peninsula have chosen fish and grass and berries as their main diet of food, varied with an occasional caribou, a seal, or meal from the carcass of a dead whale or walrus washed up on the beach. During most of the months of the year, the streams are choked with salmon, affording him an inexhaustible supply until well into the middle of the winter. And as hibernation is for the most part only an alternative for existing under winter conditions, when it is hard or sometimes impossible to get food, and as the Alaska Peninsula is in winter moderated by the warming Japan Current, making it a quite mild and livable heath for old Gyas, he is forced to spend but a relatively short period in the "long sleep." This increased activity, together with the abundance of fine food, accounts for the unusual size to which the bears of that district grow.

And he is very much aware of his size and strength; and the fact that he has had no outside natural enemy through the line of his ancestors has made him aggressive, haughty and overbearing, fearing nothing and crushing all that impedes his way.

Thus, the Alaska Peninsula grizzly is to be found a most unscrupulous fighter, and his acquaintance with man and his high-powered rifles is as yet too short and limited to have impressed upon his brute mind that here is a most powerful mortal enemy. He usually charges when wounded, more than frequently when a female with very young cubs is suddenly surprised or attacked, and occasionally when watching a fresh "kill" or "cache," and surprised. And, if old Gyas decides to fight, woe betide our bold Nimrod unless he is a good shot and nonexcitable, or accompanied by someone who possesses these valuable faculties. For a wounded grizzly will not stop for one to reload his gun, nor pause to be shot at until the vital spot is struck. He means blood! Fifty bullets that are not placed in the proper spot will not stop him; and you can't back out once he accepts your challenge. Not that one is certain of being charged by every Alaskan grizzly that he fells; I have had even females retreat until knocked down. But these cases are really the exception, and the experiences of practically all the old bear hunters of that district—I have known most of them—will bear me out in the statement that these Alaskan grizzlies almost invariably charge under the three circumstances I have cited. The natives of Alaska do not often go to look for these big bears. They have a great deal of respect for them—as all others who know them have.

We are at King Cove, a native village near the site of the once famous village of Belkovski, center of the sea otter hunting grounds of old. We are about 600 miles southwest of Kodiak, the nearest town of over fifteen white inhabitants; and very near the extreme western end of the Alaska Peninsula, and almost due north of Honolulu by location. And here, where the traveler is almost never seen, we will start out to hunt for the biggest of carnivora—start it by incidentally being shipwrecked, almost drowned and getting a foot severely frozen.

It was on the morning of Wednesday, November 1, 1916, that I left King Cove in a 28-foot covered-over powerboat with Captain Charlie Madsen. We headed for the Isanotski Straits, at the end of the peninsula, and the Bering Sea country, where I intended hunting Grant's Barren Ground caribou and the big grizzlies at several desirable localities near the end of the peninsula.

It was cloudy; looked like another snowstorm; but the wind being from the north, rave it might and the low hills of the mainland would protect us until we reached the end of the peninsula, where we could hunt bear and wait for more favorable winds. But the winds of the North are most fickle!

It was a most magnetic sight as we plied out towards the cape at the entrance of the bay, sending flock after flock of salt-water ducks flopping off over the swelling surface of the blue-green sea. An occasional seal could be seen plunging headlong into the water from the jut of a reef or an outcrop of the rocky shoreline. The hills were gray, dappled with the first settling snows of winter, and the clouds were heavy and leaden looking.

As we rounded the cape the swells became more pronounced, carrying a deep, rolling, green-sided trough. But our boat plied steadily on, plunging its nose fearlessly into the rising waves.

Breasting some five miles of rocky coastline, we rounded the second cape at the entrance to Cold (Morofski) Bay, which protrudes some twenty-five miles back into the peninsula, almost making what is to the west an island and what is to the east the end of the peninsula. As we had expected, the wind was raging out of the bay to seaward. But heading the boat's nose towards Thin Point, about ten miles distant, we started fighting our way to the protection of the opposite cape.

Madsen had been watching the sky with misgiving and shortly announced that the wind was changing to the southwest.

I naturally inquired what would be the best course to pursue, knowing that it undoubtedly meant more storm and that we would soon be in the thick of it.

"Cap" decided we would take a chance on reaching Thin Point before the wind had swung to the southwest and thrown the storm in our faces. Once behind the cape we would be safe.

But we were not halfway across when the wind, swinging out past the protection of the peninsula and clashing against the tide, was soon lashing the sea into a stormy havoc. Diving into one great swell, the wind toppled its crest over the boat, washing overboard the hatch-cover and pouring a volume of water into the hold upon our supplies and outfit. I got on deck and endeavored to get a piece of canvas nailed over the open hatchway before another big one should pour its volume into the boat, at the same time clinging as best I could to the pitching vessel.

In the midst of all this, and as if to impress more forcibly upon us our insignificance in this big affair, our engine stopped. Gas engines are hellish things anyhow, and always buck in just the wrong place. But one must act quickly in a case such as this, and almost before I knew it the boat's sail was up and we were racing back before the wind, toward the entrance to the bay we had not long left.

I took the rope and wheel, while Madsen endeavored to get the engine running again, though vainly.

But the wind was now coming in such gusts that each one nigh turned our boat onto its nose. It was also snowing and sleeting, almost hiding the outline of the coast.

A gust hit our sail, turning the boat clear on its side, taking water over the rail, and we narrowly escaped finding ourselves in the arms of Neptune himself. Madsen left the engine and decided we would run before the wind and tack into King Cove Bay.

We crossed the entrance to the bay, driven at top speed towards the opposite cape and line of rocky reefs.

Going as close to as safe, the sail was drawn in with an endeavor to throw it to the opposite side, thus turning the boat. But the wind was too strong and the sea too rough, and try as we might, we would only be driven helplessly on towards the reef where the waves were dashing their foam and spray high in the air. Then a big wave took the flopping sail, pulling the boat over onto its side until the canvas was torn from end to end. As a last resort the anchor was thrown out; this failed to catch sufficiently to hold us and was regained at great difficulty when we saw that hitting the reef was inevitable.

The first rock of the reef that the boat hit, jammed its head through the bottom of the hull and we clambered out into the big dory we were towing and started for shore through the narrow, raging channels in the reef. But this being an open boat, it soon swamped in the breakers and we were forced to take to the water and make shore as best we could. Swimming was impossible, but keeping our heads above the water as best we could, and riding the waves, we were soon washed up on the rocky shore, like half-drowned rats.

To build a fire was impossible for lack of material; we must wait until the boat washed over the reef and was driven ashore. So, wet and cold, and facing a biting snow and sleet and rain-pelleted wind, we walked back and forth over the rocks and waited.

Through all this, while we had been battling with the elements for our very lives, I had noticed with no small interest how very little the storming and havoc had inconvenienced the little creatures that made their homes in or on the sea. The ducks swam about, quacking, and apparently thoroughly enjoying their buoyant existence. So even storms at sea, it seemed, were a mere matter of relativity and part of the everyday life of those that made their home thereon.

Eventually the boat came ashore—it was fortunately high tide—and getting aboard we got out block and tackle, sunk our anchor as a deadman, and pulled the boat up as best we could. Supplies and everything were drenched and several planks in the hull were smashed.

When we had done all that we could we started for the village—a hard hike. It was well after dark when we reached the squatty barrabaras, or native dirt huts, of King Cove, and we were wet and tired and miserable—ready for a meal and the blankets.

As I began to thaw out, however, I found that part of my right foot had frozen—the leather boots I had been wearing having shrunk and stopped the circulation of blood, causing the freezing. I was laid up for over a week with my foot, though it took Madsen, with the assistance of several natives, somewhat longer to get the boat repaired and back to the village.

Such are but a bit of the "pleasures" that often come with hunting big bear at the western end of the Alaskan Peninsula.

I was especially fortunate in making a one-day bag of four of these Alaska Peninsula bears, a big female and her three yearling cubs, the latter being as large as quite mature Southern brown bears I have gotten.

Deciding to spend a day alone in the hills after caribou, I took the .30–40 Winchester—in consideration of the bear—and followed the beach of a lagoon or bay to its head about two and half miles from the village. From the head of the lagoon a valley rose at an easy pitch for about two miles to a low divide on the opposite side of which was a large valley extending out onto the Pacific. This was a very good place for caribou.

At the head of the lagoon I stopped to shoot some salt water ducks with a .22 Colt revolver, but had fired but a few shots when I was attracted by the bawling of a bear. Glancing in the direction of the sound, I saw a brown bear making a speedy, somewhat noisy, getaway up through the alders from where he had been no doubt eating salmon in the creek a few hundred yards up-valley from me. He was then a good five hundred yards distant and in the alders. I fired, hoping at least to turn him back down the hillside, but he made the top of the ridge and went over it out of sight. I started a speedy climb up through the alders towards the top, not far from where he went over. By the time I reached this, Mr. Ursus had gone down the other side and was making a "hiyu clattewa" along the opposite side of the valley. I started up the ridge toward an open space in the alders with the intent of hurrying down to the creek and descending it with hopes of heading the bear off or getting a shot at him while crossing a wide rock slide a few hundred yards below. But I had not gone a dozen steps when I saw three other bears coming along at a good pace on quite the same course that Number One had taken. This was somewhat more of a "bear party" than I had really anticipated inviting myself to!

I felt quite certain that they would cross a small saddle through which the previous one had passed, and I decided to wait until they had come out of this and were somewhat below me before chancing a shot. I was alone, I remembered.

Squatting down in the alders, I waited with gun ready and, I must say, nerves tense. The first one to come through the saddle was the old female, a big, high-shouldered brute that strode in a manner indicating it was looking for me every bit as much as I was waiting for it. She was followed by her other two yearlings—big fellows almost as tall and as broad as they were long. Being alone, and feeling that the female would undoubtedly fight, I deemed it most wise to play doubly safe. Conditions were fortunately in my favor. The wind was from seaward, and the alders were heavy enough to conceal me from her none too good eyesight, and it would be difficult for her to determine from just which direction the report of my rifle came. The dispatching of the old one was of course my first move. The rest would be comparatively easy. I did not have an opportunity of a good shot, however, until the three had reached the creek bed and crossed and started up along the other side. I slipped into a heavy clump of alders and waited. She was not then, I was quite sure, aware of my whereabouts at least. She lumbered slowly along, yet ever watchful, I could see. Coming out in a little open space she stopped and made an apparent survey of the surrounding vicinity. I took a coarse bead and let drive at her shoulder. I could fairly hear the bullet slap into her. With a nasal bellow she wheeled and made a vicious swipe at the nearest yearling. I fired again, at which she wheeled and charged madly along the hillside opposite me. She went into a small ravine and in a moment came up into sight on one side and stopped, snout swaying high in the air to catch a scent of the danger. I steadied my aim and at the report she went down in a heap and rolled out of sight. "A bull's-eye!" I thought, and breathed a sigh of relief.

The two cubs had made off in the opposite direction, stopping occasionally to look about. I knocked down one of these at the second shot, breaking his back, though he raised on his forelegs and bawled for all he was worth. I was about to let him have another, when out of the ravine came Mrs. Ursus, mad and apparently as much alive as ever, although dragging her right foreleg. She scrambled through the alders straight to the bawling cub. Greatly surprised, and a little uneasy, I again let drive at her. She threw her head to one side, at the same time letting forth another nasal cry. At my next shot she wheeled completely around and charged along the mountainside for a short distance with head held high and every nerve strained to its utmost to locate the cause of her molestation—snarling and bawling in a manner that made me perspire uncomfortably. She was desperate and no doubt calling upon the souls of all her past ancestors to assist her in locating the peculiar new enemy. Then she charged back to the cub. Finally she made a dash almost straight in my direction.

One does not fully appreciate the thrills of real bear hunting until he has experienced just such circumstances as this. To be alone in such a case is a quite different matter from being in company—poor though it may be.

She at last came to a standstill, standing half sidelong to me, and I clamped the gold bead square on her neck and let drive. She went down, got up, and tearing a few alders up by the roots, unwillingly sank in a heap. She had finished her career as a big brown bear on the Alaska Peninsula.

The rest was quite easy and uneventful.

With the assistance of three natives I skinned the four, took the necessary measurements for mounting, and brought the pelts in by boat. The natives, however, made a second trip, bringing in every bit of the meat of all four, salting it down for winter use. The pelts were in fine condition and beautiful specimens, the large one measuring a full ten feet. They are now in the Ohio State Museum.

It was on Sunday, November 19, 1916, that I bagged the original "bearcat"—one of the largest bears ever killed on the continent.

We were hunting around the eastern side of Frosty Peak, a high volcanic mountain towering between Morzhovi and Morofski Bays and about ten miles from the Pacific. This is about twenty miles from King Cove, near the end of the peninsula, and a very good place for big bears. It was a big one that I wanted now; and though numerous tracks and one medium-sized bear were seen, none were bothered until the original "bearcat" was found. That took two days under Old Frosty.

I had previously been hunting Grant's Barren Ground caribou on the Bering Sea side of the peninsula and before we landed at the foot of Frosty Peak on our return there was a good twelve inches of snow on the ground. In places it had already drifted to a depth of five feet. Bear hunting was quite an easy matter—though a little unpleasant on account of the snow and cold—as it was a small matter to track the animals. As the streams were still open and full of salmon, but a small percentage of the bruins had sought their winter quarters, the pads of their big clawed feet having beaten paths along the iced shores of the stream where they came periodically to gorge themselves.

It was late afternoon of the second day under Frosty Peak that we found the fresh trail of our longed-for quarry. We had been investigating the broad alder-patched table of one of the valleys that cut up toward the pinnacle of Old Frosty. There were numerous tracks along the creek where the brownies had been feasting on the silver salmon, though no fresh ones of a really large bear. But as we came well up to the head of the valley we saw the well-distinguished trail of an unquestionably large bear where it had made its way up through the snow on the mountainside into a heavy growth of alders. This was at the very foot of the peak and in the highest growth of alders. Upon reaching the tracks we were well satisfied that they could have been made only by the paw and claw of just the bear that we were seeking. Although it was evident that he had been in no special hurry in making the climb, yet it was all that a six-foot man could possibly do to step from one track to the next.

To the left of the alder patch was a comparatively open track of rocky ground with only a spare patch of brush here and there. It was certain that he could not, if still in the thicket, escape in that direction without being noticed. But on the right there was a low ridge, the opposite side of which dipped down into a deep wide ravine. The alders extended to within a few yards of this ridge, and to see the other side it was necessary to mount to the top of it. Also, it was quite probable that the bear had already gone over this ridge and might then be high up in the canyon near to its hibernation quarters.

Being unable to locate the bear with my glasses, I decided to make a complete detour around the patch, to be assured whether or not he was still in there.

So leaving Charlie on the flat below, I took the two natives and started up through the alders on the trail of old Ursus. As soon as possible we mounted the ridge at the right and went along the extent of it to assure ourselves that the bear had not crossed. This he had not. But to make doubly sure that he was still in the alder patch, we went above and around it to complete the circle about the place. He was without question lying somewhere in that thicket.

Upon reaching the flat, and as a last resource, we fired several volleys up through the alders. Then one of the natives spotted him standing in a thick growth of the alders, where he had gotten up and was looking inquiringly down at us. We moved down opposite to him and I fired from the shoulder. He started off along the mountainside, like an animal that had just broken from its cage. Then I fired again. Mounting a little knoll in the open he peered dubiously down at us—in unmistakable defiance. I held on him full in the chest for my next shot, at which he let out a bellow and came for us. My shots had hit, though he had not so much as bit or clawed at the wound on either occasion—merely jumped slightly. He was then about 200 yards distant, though I was well aware of the short time that it would take him to cover that distance. And he was a big fellow—looked literally more like a load of hay than a bear, coming down the mountainside.

I had previously told the others not to shoot until I called for help, as I was anxious to fell this big brute single-handed. But on he came, and though try as I might, I could not stop him. My shots seemed to be taking no effect whatever. And then, when he had come about half the distance, I yelled "Shoot!" And I'd have liked to have done so long before. The four guns spoke simultaneously, but old Gyas still kept coming.

I squatted down in the snow, and resting my elbows on my knees, decided to take the long chance—a shot for the head. I was confident that Madsen could stop him before he reached us, and determined to take a chance shot of dropping him in a heap. The two natives, however, were not so confident and began to move backward, shooting as they went.

He turned an angle to cross a small ravine, and while he was mounting the opposite side at a decreased pace I held just forward of the snout. The first shot missed, as I saw a small flit of snow where it hit just in front of him. But at the second shot he dropped in a heap, falling on his belly with his nose run into the snow. After waiting for some moments to make certain he was beyond the trouble point, we climbed up through the alders to where he lay. The others stood by with guns ready while I went up and poked him with the end of my own gun. He was dead.

This had all taken but a few moments, though relatively it seemed a great deal longer.

He was indeed a big fellow—a genuine bearcat. We gutted him, and as it was then getting late, hit for camp. The next morning we went back to skin the animal—and no small task it was!

He had been hit twelve times, we found. Nine of the shots had entered the neck and shoulder and two in the head and one in the abdomen. One bullet had hit him squarely in the mouth, shattering the tops of his lower teeth on one side, piercing the tongue and lodging in the back of his throat. Four of the .30 caliber leads were retrieved from the shoulder, where they had not so much as reached the bone. The shot that stopped him struck well up on the brain box, but squarely enough to break the casing of the bone and penetrate the skull, though only a part of the lead entered the brain, the most of it spattering off in the fleshy part of the head. It was a lucky shot on an even more lucky day!

We estimated his live weight at from 1,600 to 1,800 pounds, and the skin at twelve feet in length. The actual measurements of the tanned skin, however, as made by Chas. A. Ziege, noted taxidermist of Spokane, Wash., are: eleven feet four inches maximum length, by ten feet six inches spread of fore legs. The skull, measured one year after killing, eighteen and one-quarter inches, or one-half inch under the world record, according to Washington, DC, authorities.

CHAPTER TEN

Grizzly Attack Survival Epic

Lamar Underwood

MY PREVIEW OF THE REVENANT *MOVIE TALKS ABOUT THE BIG-BUDGET epic when it was soon to be released. It features the betrayal of leaving Hugh Glass for dead, a drama that comes alive again in film.*

Before covered wagons crossed the plains, carrying pioneer settlers who dreamed of the lands beyond the distant mountains . . .

Before cowboys drove herds of cattle, eating dust and shouting "yippee-ki-yay" . . .

Before prospectors panned remote mountain creeks for pay-dirt . . .

Long before these epic events were notched as icons in the history of the frontier mountain west, men with special skills and burning desires made their way into the peaks—into the vast unknown where only the footprints of native Americans had ever marked the passage of men. Today these early explorers are called "Mountain Men." Their adventures, on their own in the great untouched wilderness, with hostile Indians a constant danger, are the stuff of a gigantic mass of legends, literature, and film.

These were bearded rough-hewn men, wearing greasy buck-skins, carrying muzzle-loading rifles and toting packs containing what they called "possibles"—which meant gear they might need. Everything from flint and steel to bullets and a spare knife. They knew how to be at home in the wilds, capable of doing everything from following a set of elk tracks to building a shelter—or even a cabin. They talked funny, with expressions like "Waugh!" meaning delight or disgust; "went under" for dying; "rubbed out" for killed by Indians; and calling themselves "this coon," or "this child," or "this nigger." Even though they travelled and hunted in groups at times, for protection from raids by the native tribes, they were essentially loners. They had turned their backs on civilization, left the settlements of other men as far behind them as possible.

A life "loose and free's as any animal" as novelist A. B. Guthrie puts it in *The Big Sky*.

Such a life did not come without a price.

* * *

Hugh Glass is crawling again.

Out of the dusty pages of history, out of the visions created by legends, mountain man Hugh Glass has been restored to life. On movie screens throughout the United States and the world, in a feature film as big and colorful as they come, the story of Hugh Glass is unfolding before our very eyes.

Hugh Glass crawling through the wilderness on the screen is portrayed by the actor Leonardo DiCaprio in the movie *The Revenant*, the biggest and most realistic mountain man movie since *Jeremiah Johnson*. Just as happened in real life, back in 1823, Hugh Glass is literally crawling for survival. He is near death from the horrific wounds of a grizzly attack. The bear's claws have slashed the mountain man's body like sword blades, and the beast has taken great bites into Glass's body, even his head. Glass is so far gone that his two mountain man companions have given him up for dead. Not only have they left him alone, one of them has helped himself to Glass's rifle and all his gear.

Hugh Glass is not dead. He isn't "very much alive," as the expression goes, but he is able to crawl. This is exactly what he does, with hopes of somehow clinging to life and making his way to Fort Kiowa, some two hundred miles distant on the Missouri river in what is now South Dakota. As he crawls, he is fueled by his desire to live and a raging need to take revenge on the men who have betrayed him.

The movie that puts this Hugh Glass drama—and much more—on the screen is based on the novel with the same title by Michael Punke, originally published in 2002 and re-published by Picador in 2015.

As a self-confessed addict of everything "mountain man"— from books and film to TV reality shows—I have been hooked by the action, scope, and filmmaking splendor I see in *The Revenant* previews. The obvious questions spring into mind: Is this movie as good as *Jeremiah Johnson*? Will it treat the Hugh Glass legend fairly?

Since "revenant" is a word that I've never heard or used in my life, I had to hit the dictionary to learn it means "one that returns after death or a long absence." The storytelling promise in those words has attracted other writers and filmmakers before *The Revenant*. Hugh Glass's epic crawl and fight for life and revenge inspired the novel *Lord Grizzly* by Frederick Manfred and the movie *Man in the Wilderness* (1971). A half-dozen or so nonfiction books are devoted to the Hugh Glass saga.

My interest in mountain men has led me to write some magazine articles about them and to edit an entire book, *Tales of the Mountain Men* (2004). That book includes a chapter on Hugh Glass, an excerpt from *Lord Grizzly*.

Now *The Revenant* has my interest in Hugh Glass boiling over with new enthusiasm. Even before seeing the film, I have wanted to learn everything I could about the movie production. And I have wanted to know more about the man himself.

The producers of *The Revenant* make no claim that the film is a "true story," one that actually happened just as shown. The subtitle on *The Revenant* says, "Inspired by True Events." Michael Punke instructs readers the same way in the original novel. That's fair enough, because the details of Hugh Glass's early life are clouded with mystery. The events of the grizzly attack and its aftermath are well documented, however. Hugh Glass did survive his injuries in a trek of survival and revenge that are now part of our frontier history.

Although "the crawl" is a high point in the Hugh Glass drama, both the movie and his real life, Hugh Glass was no tenderfoot. We know today that his background was a mixture of myths, exaggerations, and a few hard and proven facts. We know for sure that by the time he ran into the nightmare grizzly, at forty-three he was a veteran of Indian fights and had the hunting and trapping skills that made the mountain men self-sufficient.

Despite the sketchy details of his youth, we are told Hugh Glass was born in Pennsylvania in 1780. Legends, unsubstantiated, of his early years include the colorful, folk-hero tale of being captured by privateers commanded by Jean Lafitte. He is said to have been forced to be a pirate for two years, then escaped in 1819 in the area of what today is Galveston, Texas.

Glass and a fellow escapee were resourceful and lucky enough to survive a trek north, through hostile Indian country. But their luck ran out in what is now Kansas, when a band of Pawnees captured them. As Glass watched, they commenced their favorite form of torture on his friend, pushing tiny sticks of fat pine into his body, from the feet on up. When they set fire to the lower sticks, the flames spread rapidly and made the body into a human torch.

Glass talked his way out of this fate, it is said, by begging the chief to accept a gift that had gone unseen in his pockets. The rare package of cinnabar, which makes brilliant red paint, saved his life. He lived several years with the Pawnees, learning their skills of survival, living on the land, an adopted son of the tribe. He no doubt fought with the Pawnees against enemy tribes, but attacks on white men are not recorded. His life with the Pawnees ended in 1822 when he joined his chief on a journey to St. Louis to smoke a peace pipe with the superintendent of Indian affairs, William Clark, of Lewis and Clark fame. Glass left the tribe here, a loner without any ties, his eyes still turned from his native Pennsylvania to the mountains of the Upper Missouri.

Whether or not that happened as described, we do know for certain that in 1823 in St. Louis he saw this ad in the January 16 *Missouri Republican*:

For the Rocky Mountains
The subscribers wish to engage One Hundred MEN,
to ascend the Missouri to the Rocky Mountains.
There to be employed as Hunters.
As a compensation to each man fit for such business,
$200 Per Annum
will be given for his services, as aforesaid.
For particulars, apply to J. V. GARMIER or W. ASHLEY,
at St. Louis. The expedition will set out for this place
on or before the first of March next.
ASHLEY and HENRY

General William Ashley was the expedition's organizer and leader, and Captain Andrew Henry was in charge of the advance brigade. Ashley's "One Hundred MEN" now included several names that would eventually include a Mountain Man Hall of Fame, including Jim Bridger, then seventeen. Hugh Glass was there.

In late August, the advance party was encamped on the Grand River, in what is present-day Perkins County, South Dakota, rerouting their path to the Upper Missouri by way of the Yellowstone. Earlier that summer, one of their groups had lost sixteen men in an attack by the Arikara (Ree) tribe. They had retaliated with a murderous raid on the Arikara in which they had been supported by troops from Fort Leavenworth and warriors from the Arikara's deadliest enemy, the Sioux. Henry's unit was to keep pushing toward the Upper Missouri to open the fur trade, while waiting for a second expedition from General Ashley to rendezvous with them the following spring and bring out the furs.

On August 23, Hugh Glass was hunting, carrying his beloved and trusty Kentucky flintlock, an Anstadt, .53 caliber, capable of throwing a ball two hundred yards. Hunting alone, the way he always liked, Glass suddenly came upon two grizzly bear cubs. He knew instantly he was in trouble. The sow would not be far away. His fears were confirmed about the same time he got his flintlock ready. He got off a shot before she charged, but it did little good. The great bear was on him in a slashing, crashing storm of fury.

Glass was unconscious when fellow hunters from the brigade found him beneath the dead bear. One of the trappers described Glass as "tore nearly to peases." They patched him up as best they could. The group carried him in a travois for a couple of days, then Captain Henry decided Glass could not be saved. He paid two men a bonus to stay behind with Glass while the main body pressed on. Young Jim Bridger and Tom Fitzgerald—twenty-three and a hothead bully—volunteered to wait for Glass to die. They were to bury him and then catch up with the main group.

After a day or so, Glass was still breathing, but certainly seemed on the edge of death. The two men staying with him rolled him into a buffalo robe and started digging a grave. Then came an Indian attack, and Bridger and Fitzgerald bolted. They not only took off, but Fitzgerald grabbed Glass's rifle and bag of "possibles." Even his knife. They caught up with the main brigade and told Captain Henry that Hugh Glass was dead and buried.

Hugh Glass was not dead. Eventually he began to crawl, eat roots and berries, literally clawing his way over the ground like an animal. His life was probably saved when he found a buffalo carcass from a wolf kill. Eventually he could stand, and limp along. He made a crutch from a stick. Onward he continued, with visions of killing Bridger and Fitzgerald aflame in his thoughts. His journey eventually put him among friendly Sioux who helped him get to Fort Kiowa.

I have no intention of spoiling the movie for you by revealing what happened to Hugh Glass after he reached Fort Kiowa. Everyone knows Jim Bridger went on to become a legendary mountain man himself. As for Glass, I can say that he went on to other battles with Indian tribes before leaving the mountains for the southwest. Life on the Santa Fe Trail could not hold him, however, and he returned to the high-country Rockies. In the winter of 1833, Glass and a fellow trapper were ambushed by Arikara while crossing the ice of the frozen Yellowstone River. This time there was no miracle to save the life of Hugh Glass.

The movie that brings us the new revelation of the Hugh Glass legend is a big one—in every way. Reports we have seen estimate it will play two hours and thirty-one minutes long. We can see from the trailer on the internet that it is action-packed with all the color, sounds, and atmosphere of the mountain man era, and is far and away the most significant mountain man movie since *Jeremiah Johnson*. That it will be compared to *Jeremiah Johnson* is inevitable, but from what I can see from the trailers, and from information about the film gleaned from the filmmakers themselves, *The Revenant* is going to stand tall at the box office and eventually in the DVD market.

Playing Hugh Glass, Leonardo DiCaprio heads a big cast that includes Will Poulter as Jim Bridger and Tom Hardy as Tom Fitzgerald. Distributed by 20th Century Fox, the movie is a big-budget enterprise co-produced by five companies and directed by Alejandro González Iñárrtiu, academy-award-winning director of *Birdman*.

"When you see the film," promises Iñárrtiu, "you will see the scale of it. And you will say, Wow!"

That quote came from an interview with writer Kim Masters for *The Hollywood Reporter*. Such Hollywood trade publication articles point back to the difficulties in filming *The Revenant*. Shot in Alberta and in Argentina, the film's autumn setting was difficult to recreate in weather conditions that were sometimes too hot, and often too cold. The decision of director Iñárrtiu and cinematographer Emmanuel Lubezki to only shoot in natural light heightens the realism immensely, but was a tough taskmaster for filming schedules. Also, Iñárrtiu refused to use computer-generated effects.

(See our separate article for a behind-the-scenes look at making the film.)

If *The Revenant* turns out to be the successful epic it promises to be, the difficulties and budget runovers in making the film will seem worthwhile.

For me, the chance for seeing a new big-budget mountain man movie like this one will be a present I really look forward to enjoying more than once.

I already told you I'm a mountain man junkie, eager for books, film, whatever creations I can find that take my mind and spirit to the time such men roamed the mountains, "loose and free's as ary animal."

This old coon's got a taste for it. We'll find beaver, one place or 'tother. Waugh!

CHAPTER ELEVEN

The Solitary Hunter

George Bird Grinnell

GEORGE BIRD GRINNELL, 1849 TO 1938, WAS A RENOWNED HISTORIAN and naturalist whose great prose is available in several books with detailed looks at the old west, particularly buffalo days and Indian life. Here, in an excerpt from his book Beyond the Old Frontier, *he brings us experiences from a pioneer hunter from a manuscript long out of print and lost.*

In the year 1847, John Palliser, an Irishman, sailed from Liverpool by the good ship *Cambria* for an extended trip in America to make acquaintance with "our Trans-Atlantic brethren, and to extend my visit to the regions still inhabited by America's aboriginal people—now, indeed, driven far westward of their rightful territories and pressed backward into that ocean of prairies extending to the foot of the great Rocky Mountains."

Palliser was a young man of good family, the son of Colonel Wray Palliser, of Comragh, County Waterford. Like so many of his race, he was energetic, quick-witted, forceful, and possessed a great fund of humor. He seems to have been first of all a hunter, and like all successful hunters to have been a keen and close observer. Some time after his return to England he wrote a book giving his experiences of adventure in the Far West. It is one of the best books of hunting adventure ever written—terse, always to the point, modest, giving facts and conclusions, and very little about his own views of life. The book has long been out of print and is now not easily obtained, but it is really a model in the picture that it paints of old-time conditions and in the self-effacement of the author.

[Editor's Note: In the following excerpts from his book, *Beyond the Old Frontier*, author Grinnell follows his introduction of Palliser with descriptions of an excerpt from one of Palliser's great adventures in the Yellowstone region.]

This man Palliser engaged to make a trip back to Fort Union and thence on horseback up the Yellowstone River, intending at the close of the trip to make bull-hide boats and transport their skins and other effects back to Fort Union by water. For this trip two additional men were hired, a stout Canadian named Pérey and a half-breed named Paquenode. Palliser and Boucharville were to do the hunting; the other two were to keep the camp, mind the horses, and cook. In the meantime it was early in April and the wild-fowl were beginning to arrive from the South. Palliser was keen to shoot some but had no shot. He tried to manufacture it and finally did so by beating out lead quite flat, cutting it into little bars, and again cutting these into little cubes an eighth of an inch each way. These were put in a small metal boiler in the kitchen of the Fort with some smooth stones and ashes and the boiler was revolved until the sharp corners were worn off the cubes and they approached the spherical. With this imperfect ammunition, good execution was done, for of course the birds were extremely abundant.

UP THE YELLOWSTONE RIVER

The ice broke up in the Missouri on the 17th of April, and as the rising water forced up the ice, the explosion was like distant thunder. For over thirty hours the river rushed by in a furious torrent, carrying enormous blocks of ice and roaring with a splendid sound as the masses passed along, forcing everything before them.

Soon after this the party started for Fort Union. They had very little food; some dried meat, a little bag of biscuits, some coffee, and a quart bottle of molasses to sweeten the coffee. During the march they had opportunities to secure eggs from the nests of the water-fowl, which were already laying, but even with this help, on the fifth day they were reduced to one biscuit each.

Early next morning we were passing along the side of the river, very hungry, and making a short march with the intention of hunting in the afternoon. Pérey carried a double-barrelled gun loaded with buck-shot, and was walking near the pack-horse, Ishmah and his travail following me, when we were astonished by the sudden appearance of four antelopes climbing up the bank close at hand. Owing to the steepness of the bank, they did not come in sight of us until they had reached the summit; the moment they did so they wheeled round, but not before Pérey fired and shot one, which rolled down the bank into the water, and was carried down the stream.

Boucharville and I tugged at our gun-covers; his he could not remove quickly enough; I tore away the thong of mine—which had run into a knot—with my teeth, and cocked my rifle. By this time the other three antelopes were swimming away in the broad stream; a little eddy in the rapid current turned one of them broadside to me; I fired, hitting the animal between wind and water, behind the shoulder,—its head drooped, as, floating dead on the surface of the water, it was carried down the stream after its companion. Pérey then performed a splendid feat; he ran down the side of the river far enough to enable him to undress,—which he partly did in running,—jumped into the half-frozen water, along which the blocks of ice were still at intervals coursing, striking out boldly, laid his hand on the first carcass, then with great exertion reached the second as it floated by, and brought both into the bank: this was the more fortunate, for half a minute more would have swept them past the bend into the rapids beyond where the scene occurred, and involved not only the loss of our game, but a considerable risk to this brave fellow.

The two antelopes afforded us quite a sufficiency of food to last until our arrival at Fort Union, which we reached early on the ninth day after our departure from the Minitarées.

At Fort Union food was scarce. The Indians camped there were afraid to venture away from the post to hunt, and immediately about the post white hunters and Indians had been hunting until all the game had been killed or driven away.

It did not take long to get together such supplies as might be had for Palliser's party—saddles, bridles, ammunition, a couple of traps, some coffee, sugar, and salt. It was necessary to cross the Missouri River from north to south below the mouth of the Yellowstone. This done, a few miles would take them into a land of plenty, a region where game was abundant; but the crossing would be difficult. The river was high and the water still cold. While going down the river they were fortunate enough to see deer and a little later some elk, of which they secured two. Their abundance now made them think of the starvation back at Fort Union and, packing up their surplus meat, they took it back to the fort to exchange for certain much needed things. Among these things were fishhooks, awls, needles, and, most important of all, an excellent four-oared skiff.

With the boat they succeeded in taking their horses and party across the Missouri, and this done they cached their precious skiff, burying it under the willows on the south bank of the Yellowstone, close to its junction with the Missouri.

Almost at once they found themselves in a country of abundant game, and of this game the antelope chiefly impressed the author. Of them he said:

> These march in line, sometimes for several miles together, and, by imitating the movements of their leader, exhibit the most striking effects, resembling military evolutions: they simultaneously whirl round their white breasts and red flanks, like the "Right face!—Left face!" of a regiment on parade. Obedient to the motions of their leader, when he stops, all stop: he stamps and advances a step, the slight similar impulse waves all down along the line; he then gives aright wheel, and round go all their heads for one last look; finally, he gives the right face about, and away "their ranks break up like clouds before a Biscay gale." Stately wapiti wandered on the plain, feeding not far from the willows, to whose friendly shelter in they crashed the moment we presented ourselves to their view. And as we approached steep frowning cliffs, overhanging the river, I saw, for the first time, the wild sheep or grosse corne of the Rocky Mountains, balancing themselves, chamois-like, on the tops of most inaccessible crags, whither they had rushed on first catching sight of us.

He repeats the ancient fable that the sheep horns are so large and solid as to enable the animal to safely fling himself on his head from considerable heights.

He made a hunt for this new game and succeeded in killing a great ram, while Boucharville got two lambs, at this season much better food than the ram, for the sheep in early spring, feeding largely on the wild leeks, often tastes of this so strongly as to be almost uneatable.

In this land of plenty the party had a pleasant, easy time and lived like fighting-cocks. Palliser's clothing by this time was falling to pieces, and he was obliged to replace it by a coat made of an elk-skin, and trousers of the hides of blacktail deer. While in camp here Indians appeared on the other side of the river, but did not discover the hunters. However, the half-breed Paquenode, who appears to have been a natural coward, was frightened nearly to death and even tried to seize the best horse in the party in order to run away.

It was now late in May, and Palliser determined to build some boats and return to Fort Union, and then, taking up the skiff buried at the mouth of the Yellowstone, to row down to the Minitarée Fort about two hundred and eighty miles. The skeletons of the boats were made of willows, and these frames covered with bull-hides. After the canoes were loaded, Palliser and Boucharville occupied the first boat and towed the second. He sent the other men back to Fort Union with the horses.

Late one evening, as they were floating down the river, they heard voices, and presently passed an Indian camp unobserved, and landing a little below it quietly returned to the vicinity and found the party to consist of two old men, an old woman, and ten young people. After a little observation, the two white men walked into the Crow camp, where the terrified children ran away screaming. The fears of the Indians were soon allayed, for Boucharville could talk Crow, and the relations between the two parties became very cordial.

While at Fort Union Palliser sent his horses by an Indian friend down to Fort Berthold, while he, with two of his three men, raised the buried skiff and started down the river. On their way an attack was threatened by a war-party of Indians, while the men were out looking for mountain sheep. Boucharville and Palliser retreated to the camp and there took up a position in the timber, and the Indians, after some threatening demonstrations, made up their minds that the position was too strong to be attacked and moved off. Later, the travellers came upon two white trappers whose arms had become useless and who were then engaged in making bows and arrows with which to kill game. These two, Gardépée and Dauphin, were competent young men and made a valuable addition to the party. It was only the next day when Palliser, while skinning a deer that he had killed, was called by Dauphin, and as he ran toward him and passed over a hill he saw a bear standing on his hind legs looking about him, while Dauphin, hidden behind a rock, was industriously snapping his useless pistol at the bear. When he saw Palliser the bear ran, but was brought back by Dauphin, who imitated the call of a buffalo-calf, so that Palliser shot at him, but only hit him in the flank.

The bear clawed at the spot where the ball struck him, and charged up to within twenty paces of us, while I was reloading; whereupon Dauphin snapped his pistol again at him without effect. Fortunately for us, Bruin was only a two-year-old, and afraid to rush in, though large enough to have smashed both of us, defenceless as we were at the moment, and, before I could get on my percussion cap, bolted over the brow of the hill. I was still so thoroughly blown from my run over the rocky ground, that I gave up my heavy rifle to Dauphin, who threw down the useless pistol, and started in chase, I following him. He soon got a shot at the bear, who turned round, clawed at the wound, gave a savage growl, and ran into one of those little clumps which always mark a watercourse in the hilly country. I took the rifle again, loaded, and pursued the enemy right into the clump, in spite of the remonstrances of Dauphin, and, getting a sight of him first, gave him a finishing shot between eye and ear. Although he was but a young bear, only in his third year, it was with great difficulty that we could drag him out; he measured five feet four inches from rump to the muzzle, and his claws were three inches and three-quarters long. Had he been fully grown, and possessed of that amount of courage and ferocity with which the old grisly bears, both male and female, are endowed, it would certainly have fared badly with us that day. However, we skinned our prize with great satisfaction; and I was exceedingly pleased with the pluck and daring of my companion, who had been twice charged by the bear, and whose pistol had twice snapped.

A day or two later Palliser and Dauphin had a fine buffalo-chase which led them a long way. They started in pursuit of a new-born buffalo-calf, and this is what happened:

The cow, of course, went off, and at a tolerable pace, followed by the calf, at an astonishing rate for so young a beast. Dauphin wanted to shoot the mother, in order not only to shorten the race, but to increase our chance of rearing the calf, by cutting off the cow's udder when dead; but that, of course, I would not allow, and ended the discussion by knocking up the muzzle of the rifle which he was using with the barrel of my gun. Then bidding him follow my example, I threw down my gun to lighten myself, calling on Boucharville to take care of the two; and drawing our belts a hole tighter, we dashed off again up hill and down dale, till at last we stretched away right out along the prairie for five or six miles. By-and-by the little calf began to show symptoms of failing, and the cow, allowing her instinct of self-preservation to overcome her maternal attachment, made the best of her way off, and crossing some inequalities in the ground, was lost to the sight of her offspring. The little fellow then stopped; whereupon Dauphin, who possessed a wonderful facility for imitating the calls of animals, immediately began to grunt like a buffalo-cow, and to our great amusement the little beast turned about, cocked up his tail, and came galloping back to us. We then turned about, and to our great delight it frisked round us all the way into the camp. I was most anxious to get it to the fort as early as possible, for I knew that if I could do so in time, I might by chance be able to rear it on pounded Indian corn and lukewarm water.

The next day another calf was captured out of a herd which was crossing the river, and now Palliser had a pair which he hoped he might succeed in getting to Europe—as later he did. For the first day or two of their captivity these little calves were fed on strong broth, but there were domestic cows at the fort and these reared the calves.

Shortly after Palliser's arrival at the fort, Mr. Chardon died, having first requested Palliser to write his will. Boucharville, when sounded on the question of making another hunt, declared that he would go wherever Palliser wished to; and the next day they took the horses across the river with the skiff, intending to hunt up the Little Missouri River and to look for grizzly bears in the Turtle Mountains. On the fourth day of their journey from Fort Berthold they reached the Turtle Mountains. Here they found a war lodge, built by a party of Minitarées the year before, and took possession of it. Boucharville, an experienced man, did not like to remain in this debatable land, which was on the border of the Sioux and Minitarée territory, and began at once to figure on when they could get away.

Here bear, antelope, elk, and sheep were extremely abundant and food was always plentiful. One day while Palliser was beginning to skin an elk, just killed, Boucharville, who was about to clean his gun, was charged by a grizzly, and escaped her by dashing into a clump of rose-bushes. The bear, which had cubs with her, charged after Palliser, who was running toward his horse, which he feared would be lost if it smelt the bear. When he reached the horse he stopped and faced the bear, which also stopped and stood up, and then turned and ran. Palliser shot at the bear, but hit her too far back. She stopped to bite at her wound and gave him time to load again. Just as he was putting a copper cap on the nipple the bear rose on her hind legs, and he sent a bullet through her heart. Palliser was very lucky in that his horse did not pull back or shy, and that there was nothing to disturb his aim. When the horse was brought to the bear and the skin put upon him, he paid no attention and showed no signs of fear, a very unusual thing, for horses are commonly very much afraid even of bearskins.

After they reached camp Dauphin started out to capture one of the young bears, but as Palliser thought the chances of finding them were very slight he did not go with him, but afterward regretted this. Dauphin killed one of the little bears and tried to take the other alive, but it fought fiercely, tearing his clothes and cutting him with its claws. Dauphin had armed himself with a stout club, but, even so, had done no more than make a draw of the battle.

They now started back toward the Little Missouri and on the way saw a bear, which, to Palliser's very great disgust, was lost by the eagerness of Dauphin.

At the Little Missouri Palliser went duck-shooting with his smooth-bore gun, but coming on the old carcass of a bull found all about it large bear tracks, some of which looked very fresh. He drew his charges of shot and rammed down a couple of balls, and followed the tracks from the prairie until at last he discovered a large bear walking slowly along.

I approached as near as I could without his perceiving me, and, lying down, tried Dauphin's plan of imitating the lowing of a buffalo-calf. On hearing the sounds, he rose up, displaying such gigantic proportions as almost made my heart fail me; I croaked again, when, perceiving me, he came cantering slowly up. I felt that I was in for it, and that escape was impossible, even had I declined the combat; so cocking both barrels of my Trulock, I remained kneeling until he approached very near, when I suddenly stood up, upon which the bear, with an indolent roaring grunt, raised himself once more upon his hind-legs, and just at the moment when he was balancing himself previously to springing on me, I fired, aiming close under his chin: the ball passing through his throat, broke the vertebræ of the neck, and down he tumbled, floundering like a great fish out of water, till at length he reluctantly expired. I drew a long breath as I uncocked my left barrel, feeling right glad at the successful issue of the combat. I walked round and round my huge prize, surveying his proportions with great delight; but as it came on to rain, I was obliged to lose no time in skinning him. I got soaked through before I succeeded in removing his tremendous hide, and then found it too heavy for me to take away; so I was obliged to return to camp without the trophy of my conquest. It was dark when I arrived. Boucharville and Dauphin had built a most comfortable little hut of logs and bark, and having laid down the skins and spread our beds inside, with the saddles at our heads for pillows, and a good roaring fire outside at our feet, we fell heartily to our supper of elk meat and coffee.

At daybreak next morning I repaired on horseback to the scene of my conflict with the bear, and found, to my great delight, on my arrival at the spot, that neither the skin nor the carcass of the bear had been touched by the wolves. This fact confirmed to me the testimony of the hunters and trappers of these parts, as to the great awe in which the grisly bear is held by the wolves and lesser animals of prey. If a bear kills an animal, or finds a dead carcass on the prairie, he appropriates it; and though many a hungry prowler passing by may look wistfully at the choice morsel, it is like the eastern monarch's share, 'taboo'; and even when the mountain monarch is absent, the print of his paw is a seal sufficient for its security. It cost me considerable exertion to place the reeking hide on my saddle; but I succeeded at last, and climbing on the top of it, lighted my pipe and rode back into camp. Riding along, towards noon we descried another bear, a lean, hungry-looking monster, prowling about searching for *pommes blanches*, and, to judge from his appearance, likely to afford us a pretty severe fight. In approaching him, we did not take any precaution to avoid giving him our wind, concluding, from my former experience, that he would not decline the combat; but in this instance I was mistaken, for rushing away down a ravine, he was soon lost to our view. This result, although it disappointed me at the time, yet gave me a further insight into the disposition and habits of the animal, and agreed with the accounts I had heard from many hunters and trappers with whom I had previously conversed on the subject; namely, that a grisly bear will, in most instances, run away from a man on getting his wind, unless previously wounded, or under such circumstances as to make him think that he cannot escape. Old Mr. Kipp, of Fort Union, told me that once, when on one of his numerous journeys from the States, he was in the Indian country, and had gone out of camp with his double-barrelled gun to look for ducks; he was seen from a distance by a grisly bear, who came cantering towards him. The day was fine, and the old gentleman did not know which way the wind blew, but had sufficient presence of mind to pluck off some of the woolly material of which his blue blanket capote was composed, and throw it into the air; and marking the direction of the current ran a little distance round, till he got full in the line of it, and then stood bolt upright facing Bruin, who rose on his hind-legs for a moment, surveying the tough old man, and then shuffled off, shaking his head as if he considered him meat rather too savoury for his palate.

There were other adventures with grizzly bears and Palliser recounts a story told by Boucharville about a bear which sprang upon the leading bull of a herd of buffalo and killed it. Other accounts have been given of such battles where the bull killed the bear.

The time for Palliser's return was now at hand, and loading his skins into boats made of buffalo-hide he floated down the river to the Minitarée post, where James Dawson the old fur trader was now in charge. A little later, boarding the Fur Company's steamer *Martha*, he took his way with all his trophies down the river and at last reached St. Louis, and his prairie hunt was over.

CHAPTER TWELVE

A Bear Trap Gone Wrong

Captain Mayne Reid

(Exerpted from A Hunter's Feast: or, Conversations around the Camp Fire.*)*

THIS TALE IS TOLD BESIDE A CAMPFIRE, LONG AGO, WHEN GAME WAS PLEN-tiful, and hunting experiences were colorful and vivid. This adventure is typical of those described at the time. Told in backcountry dialect, the language can be difficult to follow at times, but I have found it to be worth the effort.

The story starts in the city of St Louis, towards the end of the summer of some year in the nineteenth century. Reid collects together a group of six men who would pay to take part in an expedition, camping and hunting, into the prairies. They take with them a couple of paid men, professionals who would give them very necessary guidance. They all make a pact that they would each tell a round of tales around the camp fire, such stories to be amusing and instructive.

Reid himself is something of a naturalist, as we can learn from his many other books. We are given these tales just as they are told, in good English if told by an educated man, and in the dialect of the less educated ones. This latter arrangement makes the checking of the OCR transcriptions a little difficult, but never mind.

The mode of hunting the black bear does not differ from that practised with the fox or wild cat. He is usually chased by dogs, and forced into his cave or a tree. If the former, he is shot down, or the tree, if hollow, is felled. Sometimes smoking brings him out. If he escapes to a cave, smoking is also tried; but if that will not succeed in dislodging him, he must be left alone, as no dogs will venture to attack him there.

The hunter often tracks and kills him in the woods with a bullet from his rifle. He will not turn upon man unless when wounded or brought to bay. Then his assault is to be dreaded. Should he grasp the hunter between his great forearms, the latter will stand a fair chance of being hugged to death. He does not attempt to use his teeth like the grizzly bear, but relies upon the muscular power of his arms. The nose appears to be his tenderest part, and his antagonist, if an old bear-hunter, and sufficiently cool, will use every effort to strike him there. A blow upon the snout has often caused the black bear to let go his hold, and retreat terrified!

The log trap is sometimes tried with success. This is constructed in such a way that the removal of the bait operates upon a trigger, and a large heavy log comes down on the animal removing it—either crushing it to death or holding it fast by pressure. A limb is sometimes only caught; but this proves sufficient.

The same kind of trap is used throughout the northern regions of America by the fur trappers—particularly the sable hunters and trappers of the white weasel (*Mustela erminea*). Of course that for the bear is constructed of the heaviest logs, and is of large dimensions.

Redwood related an adventure that had befallen him while trapping the black bear at an earlier period of his life. It had nearly cost him his life too, and a slight halt in his gait could still be observed, resulting from that very adventure.

We all collected around the blazing logs to listen to the trapper's story.

"Well, then," began Redwood, "the thing I'm agoin' to tell you about, happened to me when I war a younker, long afore I ever thought I was a coming out hyar upon the parairas. I wan't quite growed at the time, though I was a good chunk for my age.

"It war up thar among the mountains in East Tennessee, whar this child war raised, upon the head waters of the Tennessee River.

"I war fond o' huntin' from the time that I war knee high to a duck, an' I can jest remember killin' a black bar afore I war twelve yeer old. As I growed up, the bar had become scacer in them parts, and it wan't every day you could scare up such a varmint, but now and then one ud turn up.

"Well, one day as I war poking about the crik bottom (for the shanty whar my ole mother lived war not on the Tennessee, but on a crik that runs into it), I diskivered bar sign. There war tracks o' the bar's paws in this mud, an' I follered them along the water edge for nearly a mile—then the trail turned into about as thickety a bottom as I ever seed anywhar. It would a baffled a cat to crawl through it.

"After the trail went out from the crik and towards the edge o' this thicket, I lost all hopes of follerin' it further, as the ground was hard, and covered with donicks, and I couldn't make the tracks out no how. I had my idea that the bar had tuk the thicket, so I went round the edge of it to see if I could find whar he had entered.

"For a long time I couldn't see a spot whar any critter as big as a bar could a-got in without makin' some sort o' a hole, and then I begun to think the bar had gone some other way, either across the crik or further down it.

"I war agoin' to turn back to the water, when I spied a big log lyin' half out o' the thicket, with one eend buried in the bushes. I noticed that the top of this log had a dirty look, as if some animal had tramped about on it; an' on goin' up and squintin' at it a little closter, I seed that that guess war the right one.

"I clomb the log, for it war a regular rouster, bigger than that 'n we had so much useless trouble with, and then I scrammelled along the top o' it in the direction of the brush. Thar I seed the very hole whar the bar had got into the thicket, and thar war a regular beaten-path runnin' through the brake as far as I could see.

"I jumped off o' the log, and squeezed myself through the bramble. It war a trail easy enough to find, but mighty hard to foller, I can tell ye. Thar war thistles, and cussed stingin' nettles, and briars as thick as my wrist, with claws upon them as sharp as fish-hooks. I pushed on, howsomever, feelin' quite sartin that sich a well-used track must lead to the bar's den, an' I war safe enough to find it. In coorse I reckoned that the critter had his nest in some holler tree, and I could go home for my axe, and come back the next morning—if smoking failed to git him out.

"Well, I poked on through the thicket a good three hundred yards, sometimes crouching, and sometimes creeping on my hands and knees. I war badly scratched, I tell you, and now and then I jest thought to myself, what would be the consyquince if the bar should meet me in that narrow passage. We'd a had a tough tussel, I reckon—but I met no bar.

"At last the brash grew thinner, and jest as I was in hopes I might stumble on the bar tree, what shed I see afore me but the face o' a rocky bluff, that riz a consid'able height over the crik bottom. I begun to fear that the varmint had a cave, and so, cuss him! he had—a great black gulley in the rocks was right close by, and thar was his den, and no mistake. I could easily tell it by the way the clay and stones had been pattered over by his paws.

"Of coorse, my tracking for that day war over, and I stood by the mouth of the cave not knowin' what to do. I didn't feel inclined to go in.

"After a while I bethought me that the bar mout come out, an' I laid myself squat down among the bushes facing the cave. I had my gun ready to give him a mouthful of lead, as soon as he should show his snout outside o' the hole.

"'Twar no go. I guess he had heard me when I first come up, and know'd I war thar. I laid still until 'twar so dark I thought I would never find my way back agin to the crik; but, after a good deal of scramblin' and creepin' I got out at last, and took my way home.

"It warn't likely I war agoin' to give that bar up. I war bound to fetch him out o' his boots if it cost me a week's hunting. So I returned the next morning to the place, and lay all day in front o' the cave. No bar appeared, an' I went back home a cussin'.

"Next day I come again, but this time I didn't intend to stay. I had fetched my axe with me wi' the intention of riggin' up a log trap near the mouth o' the cave. I had also fetched a jug o' molasses and some yeers o' green corn to bait the trap, for I know'd the bar war fond o' both.

"Well, I got upon the spot, an' makin' as leetle rumpus as possible, I went to work to build my trap. I found some logs on the ground jest the scantlin, and in less than an hour I hed the thing rigged an' the trigger set. 'Twan't no small lift to get up the big log, but I managed it wi' a lever I had made, though it took every pound o' strength in my body. If it come down on the bar I knew it would hold him.

"Well, I had all ready except layin' the bait; so I crawled in, and was fixin' the green yeers and the 'lasses, when, jest at that moment, what shed I hear behind me but the 'sniff' o' the bar!

"I turned suddenly to see. I had jest got my eye on the critter standin' right in the mouth o' his cave, when I felt myself struck upon the buttocks, and flattened down to the airth like a pancake!

"At the first stroke I thought somebody had hit me a heavy blow from behind, and I wish it had been that. It war wusser than that. It war the log had hit me, and war now lying with all its weight right across my two leg's. In my hurry to git round I had sprung the trigger, and down comed the infernal log on my hams.

"At fust I wan't scared, but I war badly hurt. I thought it would be all right as soon as I had crawled out, and I made an attempt to do so. It was then that I become scared in airnest; for I found that I couldn't crawl out. My legs were held in such a way that I couldn't move them, and the more I pulled the more I hurt them. They were in pain already with the heavy weight pressin' upon them, and I couldn't bear to move them. No more could I turn myself. I war flat on my face, and couldn't slew myself round any way, so as to get my hands at the log. I war fairly catched in my own trap!

"It war jest about then I began to feel scared. Thar wan't no settlement in the hul crik bottom but my mother's old shanty, an' that were two miles higher up. It war as unlikely a thing as could happen that anybody would be passing that way. And unless some one did I saw no chance of gettin' clar o' the scrape I war in. I could do nothin' for myself.

"I hollered as loud as I could, and that frightened the bar into his cave again. I hollered for an hour, but I could hear no reply, and then I war still a bit, and then I hollered again, an' kept this up pretty much for the hul o' that blessed day.

"Thar wan't any answer but the echo o' my own shoutin', and the whoopin' of the owls that flew about over my head, and appeared as if they war mockin' me.

"I had no behopes of any relief comin' from home. My ole mother had nobody but myself, and she wan't like to miss me, as I'd often stayed out a huntin' for three or four days at a time. The only chance I had, and I knew it too, war that some neighbour might be strayin' down the crik, and you may guess what sort o' chance that war, when I tell you thar wan't a neighbour livin' within less than five mile o' us. If no one come by I knew I must lay there till I died o' hunger and rotted, or the bar ate me up.

"Well, night come, and night went. 'Twar about the longest night this child remembers. I lay all through it, a sufferin' the pain, and listening to the screechin' owls. I could a screeched as loud as any of them if that would a done any good. I heerd now and then the snuffin' o' the bar, and I could see thar war two o' them. I could see thar big black bodies movin' about like shadows, and they appeared to be gettin' less afeerd o' me, as they come close at times, and risin' up on their hind-quarters stood in front o' me like a couple o' black devils.

"I begun to get afeerd they would attack me, and so I guess they would a-done, had not a circumstance happened that put them out o' the notion.

"It war jest grey day, when one o' them come so clost that I expected to be attacked by him. Now as luck would have it, my rifle happened to be lyin' on the ground within reach. I grabbed it without saying a word, and slewin' up one shoulder as high as I could, I was able to sight the bar jest behind the fore leg. The brute wan't four feet from the muzzle, and slap into him went wad and all, and down he tumbled like a felled ox. I seed he war as dead as a buck.

"Well, badly as I war fixed, I contrived to get loaded again, for I knowed that bars will fight for each other to the death; and I thought the other might attack me. It wan't to be seen at the time, but shortly after it come upon the ground from the direction of the crik.

"I watched it closely as it shambled up, having my rifle ready all the while. When it first set eyes on its dead comrade it gave a loud snort, and stopped. It appeared to be considerably surprised. It only halted a short spell, and then, with a loud roar, it run up to the carcass, and sniffed at it.

"I hain't the least o' a doubt that in two seconds more it woulda-jumped me, but I war too quick for it, and sent a bullet right plum into one of its eyes, that come out again near the back o' its neck. That did the business, and I had the satisfaction to see it cowollop over nearly on top o' the other 'n.

"Well, I had killed the bars, but what o' that. That wouldn't get me from under the log; and what wi' the pain I was sufferin', and the poor prospect o' bein' relieved, I thought I mout as well have let them eat me.

"But a man don't die so long as he can help it, I b'lieve, and I determined to live it out while I could. At times I had hopes and shouted, and then I lost hope and lay still again.

"I grew as hungry as a famished wolf. The bars were lying right before me, but jest beyond reach, as if to tantylise me. I could have ate a collop raw if I could a-got hold of it, but how to reach it war the difeeculty.

"Needcesity they say is the mother o' invention; and I set myself to invent a bit. Thar war a piece o' rope I had brought along to help mewi' the trap, and that I got my claws on.

"I made a noose on one end o' it, and after about a score o' trials I at last flung the noose over the head o' one o' the bars, and drew it tight. I then sot to work to pull the bar nearer. If that bar's neck wan't well stretched I don't know what you'd call stretchin', for I tugged at it about an hour afore I could get it within reach. I did get it at last, and then with my knife I cut out the bar's tongue, and ate it raw.

"I had satisfied one appetite, but another as bad, if not wusser, troubled me. That war thirst—my throat war as dry as a corn cob, and whar was the water to come from. It grew so bad at last that I thought I would die of it. I drawed the bar nearer me, and cut his juglar to see if thar war any relief from that quarter. Thar wan't. The blood war froze up thick as liver. Not a drop would run.

"I lay coolin' my tongue on the blade o' my knife an' chawin' a bullet, that I had taken from my pouch. I managed to put in the hul of the next day this away, now and then shoutin' as hard as I could. Towards the evenin' I grew hungry again, and ate a cut out o' the cheek o' the bar; but I thought I would a-choked for want o' water.

"I put in the night the best way I could. I had the owls again for company, and some varmint came up and smelt at the bars; but was frightened at my voice, and run away again. I suppose it war a fox or wolf, or some such thing, and but for me would a-made a meal off o' the bar's carcass.

"I won't trouble you with my reflexshuns all that night; but I can assure ye they war anything but pleasant. I thought of my ole mother, who had nobody but me, and that helped to keep up my spirits. I determined to cut away at the bar, and hold out as long as possible.

"As soon as day broke I set up my shoutin' again, restin' every fifteen minutes or so, and then takin' afresh start. About an hour after sun-up, jest as I had finished a long spell o' screechin', I thought I heerd a voice. I listened a bit with my heart thumpin' against my ribs. Thar war no sound; I yelled louder than ever, and then listened. Thar war a voice.

"Damn ye! what are ye hollowin' about?' cried the voice.

"I again shouted 'Holloa!'

"'Who the hell's thar?' inquired the voice.

"'Casey!' I called back, recognising the voice as that of a neighbour who lives up the crik; 'for God's sake this way.'

"'I'm a-comin',' he replied; "Taint so easy to get through hyar—that you, Redwood? What the hell's the matter? Damn this brush!'

"I heard my neighbour breakin' his way through the thicket, and strange I tell ye all, but true it is, I couldn't believe I war goin' to get clar even then until I seed Casey standin' in front o' me.

"Well, of coorse, I was now set free again, but couldn't put a foot to the ground. Casey carried me home to the shanty, whar I lay for wellnigh six weeks, afore I could go about, and damn the thing! I han't got over it yet."

So ended Redwood's story.

Chapter Thirteen

The Happy Hooligan

Portrait of the Black Bear

William H. Wright

WILLIAM H. WRIGHT, 1856 TO 1934, SPENT A GREAT DEAL OF HIS LIFE in the field studying black bears. His voluminous knowledge and observations are shared in his book, The Black Bear. *The excerpt provided here is but a portion of his great book. You will not see black bears in many of the attack scenarios typical of grizzly bears. The two bears are vastly different, but black bears have indeed been involved in attacks, as documented by writer Stephen Herrero in his book* Bear Attacks: Their Cause and Avoidance, *now in its third edition with Lyons Press.*

In this chapter I purpose to bring together in some sort of order the characteristic habits of the Black Bear as I have personally observed him during many years of life in the open. Of course it is never possible to watch a single wild animal from the time it is born until it grows up, lives its natural life out, and dies; nor even to follow one through the activities of an ordinary year of its life. And even if one could do this, one would have to be very careful not to generalize too broadly from the actions of a single individual. But by the time one has seen thousands of Black Bear, let us say, in many parts of their range, in all stages of growth, at all seasons of the year, in undisturbed enjoyment of their liberty, and free to follow their own instincts of work and play, one is able, by putting two and two together, to piece out a pretty accurate knowledge of the species.

One gets, also, a good working understanding of what traits are characteristic of all the normal specimens of the race, of what habits are dependent upon local conditions and vary as these alter, and of what actions are attributable to the personal dispositions of individual animals. For all animals are like men in this, that in minor matters their habits vary with the conditions under which they live, and that in still less noticeable ways the bearing of different individuals under similar circumstances is determined by their personal characters.

What follows in the present chapter, then, is a summing up of the general habits and race characteristics of the Black Bear; and all statements that are not qualified are, in my experience, observable of these animals wherever found.

Of course we all know that the Black Bear is an hibernating animal. That is to say that in most, if not in all, parts of its widely distributed range, it passes a portion of the year asleep and without food or drink, in a den or some sort of make-shift shelter. We shall have much to say later on about this strange habit, and about some of the queer notions people have about it, but we only mention it here because, since little bears are born during the time their mother is in winter quarters, it is necessary to establish winter quarters for them to be born in.

Black Bear cubs, then, are born in the winter den of the mother sometime from the latter half of January to the middle of March, according to the latitude and also according to the altitude of the den. The further north a bear happens to live, and the higher up in the hills it happens to live, the later the spring sets in and so the later the animal comes out of its retirement. And the cubs are born from six weeks to two months before the mother comes out.

The little Black Bears, when first born, are absurdly small and pitifully helpless. Their eyes, like those of puppies and kittens, are shut and do not open for some time. They have no teeth and are almost naked, and although the mother may weigh as much as four hundred pounds or more, the whole litter of cubs does not weigh over a couple of pounds, and single cubs vary from eight to eighteen ounces in weight, according to the number in the litter. A Black Bear will have all the way from one to four cubs at a time, and four is not at all uncommon. I have never seen but two grizzlies with four cubs, but I have seen a great many Black Bears with that many. Three, however, seems to be the common number throughout the Rocky Mountain region. Of course meeting a Black Bear in the woods with only one cub, even in the early spring, does not definitely prove that she only gave birth to one; because the others might have died or have been killed. But the records of Black Bears in captivity show that single cubs are not unknown.

The young cubs at first are delicate and for a week or two the mother never leaves them, but curls around them and keeps them warm and broods them. They seem, however, to have excellent lungs, for one can hear them whimper if one has located a bear's hiding place and approaches it after the cubs are born, an experience that I have had more than once in the mountains. The Messrs. Lodge, of Cuyahoga Falls, Ohio, have supplied their bears with artificial hibernating dens dug in the side of a hill where their bear pit is situated. These are supplied with ventilating shafts, and the owners, for a number of years, have been able to determine the exact date of the birth of a litter, by listening for the querulous voices of the cubs. These gentlemen, by the way, have endeavored in all possible regards to approximate natural conditions in furnishing accommodations for their captive animals; with the result that they have been among the few successful raisers of Black Bears. I will have occasion to refer more than once to the records which these gentlemen have kept during their twenty years' experience.

For some time, then, after the cubs are born, the family continues shut up in the winter den; but, unlike the grizzly, they frequently, toward the end, leave their shelter before they are ready to abandon it for good. I have seen cases where a Black Bear mother and cubs came out in deep snow, and after wandering about for several miles went back again for a full two weeks before coming out for good. In some cases the mother will come out on these preliminary excursions before the young are able to walk. But they do not either habitually or finally abandon the den until they can get down to the bottoms where the snow is gone and the vegetation has started sprouting. This, by the way, if you happen to live in the neighborhood, is an excellent time to keep a sharp watch on your young pigs.

At this stage the cubs weigh about five or six pounds and, although it is some months before they begin to forage at all for themselves, their development is now much more rapid. I have frequently watched old Black Bears with cubs in the early summer, but have never seen the young ones show any apparent interest in what the mother was eating, and hence I believe that in their natural state they are six or seven months old before they begin the process of being weaned. But although about the time the berries are ripe the cubs take to foraging pretty generally on their own account, they continue to nurse right through the summer and until they either den up with the mother in the fall or, as I think is more usual, until they are turned adrift by her before she herself dens up alone. In fact I have seen them, late in the year, and when they were of a size that should have made them ashamed of such dependence, pestering their mother as she walked, and getting occasional cuffs for their persistence.

Ben showed no concern whatever over grown-up bear dishes until the berry season came around, when he suddenly developed an appetite for outside board, and not only seemed to want all the various things the hills provided, but would howl lustily if he did not get them.

The Black Bear, while not much of a traveller, wanders over a fairly wide range in search of various foods in their season; yet, broadly speaking, is pretty apt to live and die in the general neighborhood of its birth. They wander both day and night, although when they are in a region where grizzlies are also to be found they are careful to disappear about the time that the latter, which are much more nocturnal in habit, may be expected to come out. When a Black Bear has young cubs she will stay for a week or two at a time in one place, and will scratch a nest or bed among the leaves or in a thicket and lie up there between feeds with her youngsters.

There are few things more interesting than to watch a bear with her cubs when she thinks herself alone. They are the gayest and most playful little balls of fur, and she will let them maul her and worry her and pretend to fight her. But a Black Bear does not, as the grizzly does, talk to her cubs all the time. A grizzly will walk along through the woods with two or three cubs carrying on what appears to be a connected conversation. She grunts and whines and makes noises at them that sound as though they were full of advice and admonition. They are doubtless merely encouragement or assurances of her presence. But the Black Bear is silent except in cases of danger or emergency. Then she, too, "speaks" to her youngsters, and they never seem to be at a loss for her meaning. At any rate they go up a tree at the word of command, and come down again at the grunt that means, "All right now, come on."

As the cubs grow larger and stronger the mother wanders farther afield with them, and, from sacrificing all her time and desires to their needs and safety, comes gradually first to tolerate, and toward the end of the season rather to resent, their persistent demands upon her. One imagines that it is with a final indifference and relief that she sends them off to shift for themselves. For, like other animals, a bear, while showing the most devoted and courageous love for her children while they are helpless, has a very short-lived affection for them once they cease to need her protection. In one instance the Lodges tried the experiment of returning some half-grown cubs to their mother after a comparatively short separation, during which she and her mate had been together in the main pit. The two cubs had only been by themselves for a few weeks, and before they were finally returned to the pen with their mother they were kept for some days separated from her by nothing more than an iron grating. Yet as soon as they were put into the pit with her she seized one of them and killed it, and was starting up her exercise tree after the other which had taken refuge there when the owners interfered and rescued the youngster. Here, as I see it, was a case of artificial separation which, once the mother had accepted, placed her, as far as her own feelings went, in exactly the same frame of mind toward her cubs as though she had abandoned them in the natural course of things and their company had afterward been forced upon her.

Neither the Black Bear nor the grizzly is really a sociable animal, but free Black Bears occasionally play together, which grizzlies never seem to do. Under ordinary circumstances, however, Black Bears have a funny trick of pretending not to see each other when they meet. If one of them comes into a marshy meadow or a small open glade in the woods where one or two others are already feeding, he will make the most laughable pretence of not seeing them. He will stop at the edge of the opening and go through all the motions of examining the country, carefully looking, however, everywhere but in the direction of the other bears; all of which is vastly amusing to one familiar with the keenness of his senses and the alertness of his attention, and the practical impossibility of getting within seeing or hearing distance of him without his knowing it. Meanwhile the bears already on the ground play their part in the little comedy with all the good will in the world. They have undoubtedly been aware of the approach of the newcomer long before any human watcher of the scene could have suspected it. But they give no outward sign of being aware of the new arrival. If, however, the intruder had happened to have been a grizzly they would undoubtedly have taken to their heels or taken refuge in the nearest tree with loud puffings and snortings some minutes before he reached the scene. Yet these same bears, once they have fed their fill, will frequently go to playing together as one never sees the grizzlies do. Two of them will stand up and wrestle, roll each other over and over, chase each other about, and generally have a fine romp. As a rule, however, this sort of play takes place between bears of different sizes, and the smaller one sometimes gets well thrown about and mauled.

One of the most entertaining experiences that I ever had in the woods was connected with just such an after-dinner romp between two Black Bears. I was photographing grizzlies in the Rocky Mountains in Wyoming, and had set up my camera and flash-light apparatus near a likely looking trail. My flash-pan was placed on top of a ten-foot pole stuck in the ground under a small pine tree, and a fine wire was run from the switch that operated the apparatus across the trail and tied to a convenient bush. I had completed my arrangements about half-past four in the afternoon and had concealed myself in a mass of fallen timber some seventy-five or eighty feet away prepared to wait for dusk.

Soon after I got settled I noticed two Black Bears in a little clearing to my left and, for something to do, I set to watching them. For some time they fed quietly here and there and then they took to playing. One of them was quite a bit larger than the other, but the smaller one was game and though he got considerably the worst of the rough sport they kept the play up for quite a while. Suddenly, however, in the very midst of an excited wrestling match, the little fellow drew away, stood up on his hind legs and listened for a moment, and then went up a convenient tree, his companion following his example and taking refuge in another one. I was much interested over this turn of affairs and kept a close watch to see what was going to happen next. But, after quite a little wait, the bears seemed to make up their minds that it had been a false alarm and, coming down from their respective trees, they resumed their rough and tumble fun. Not for long, however. It was only a minute or two before they repeated their former maneuvers, and this time they appeared to have no doubt as to the imminence of danger. They had worked their way over to my side of the clearing, and when they broke for shelter the little bear took refuge in the small pine tree under which my flash-pan stood, his companion selecting a larger tree a little further away. And sure enough, almost as soon as they were well off the ground an old grizzly came stalking dignifiedly out of the woods and down the trail upon which my camera was set. But he had evidently noticed that something questionable was going on, and he walked over toward the tree where the larger bear was sitting. The latter, conscious of his advantage of position, greeted the grizzly's approach with a volley of puffs and snorts, and after looking around him in a disdainful sort of way, the grizzly sauntered over toward the smaller bear's tree, where the same performance was gone through. Here, however, the grizzly found something that aroused his curiosity more keenly than a mere Black Bear, for he discovered my pole and flash-pan. He stood up on his hind legs and easily sniffed the top of the pan and then, discovering the wire, he followed it without touching it away from the pine tree and across the trail to where it was fastened. Then, his curiosity getting the better of him, he raised one front paw and pulled the bush toward him, whereupon the charge of powder exploded with a huge puff of smoke, and as I stood up in my retreat to get a better view of the outcome I caught a glimpse with one eye of a big grizzly turning a double back somersault, while with the other I saw a small Black Bear take one desperate leap from the branches of his pine tree and disappear into the wood in huge leaps.

When the last act of this little comedy began I had risen to my feet in order to get a clear view of what took place, and when the smaller Black Bear had disappeared into the woods I saw that his larger companion had become aware of my presence. I once more concealed myself among the branches, but the Black Bear in the tree kept an eye in my direction and when, at the end of five minutes or so, the smaller bear returned cautiously to the scene of his recent discomfiture and began to coax his friend to come down and resume their play, it was amusing to watch the cross-purposes at which they found themselves. For the one up the tree who knew of my presence was afraid to come down and yet unable to explain the circumstances to the one on the ground, and he in his turn was utterly unable to make head or tail of the other's actions. He finally gave up the attempt to persuade him and wandered away into the woods, and at the end of half an hour or so the other bear, evidently with serious misgivings, came carefully down the opposite side of his tree and made off at the double quick.

The Black Bear's habits of hibernation are less rigid and apparently less developed than the grizzly's. To begin with, they are far less industrious in providing themselves with a den, and less particular in having it weatherproof and well concealed. The grizzly habitually seeks out some natural cave or shelter in the rocks, high up in the mountains, often above snow line. This he prepares for occupancy by raking into it whatever he can find in the way of leaves or dried grasses, and sometimes stops up with earth and stones such holes or openings as would expose the interior to the weather. The Black Bear is far less particular. Any old place that offers him some fair promise of protection and privacy seems good enough for him. He dens up at much lower altitudes, goes into winter quarters later and comes out much earlier. One of his favorite devices is to dig a hole under the butt end of a fallen tree, rake a few leaves into the opening, and then crawl in himself. Sometimes, when the tree is a good-sized one and the roots hold the butt of it a little clear of the ground, he is saved the trouble of digging at all and makes a sort of nest in the space beneath the trunk. At other times he will dig a hole in the soft ground, and, of course, occasionally uses caves or other natural retreats if he happens to find them handy. Ben, it will be recalled, dug under the floor of my barn when it came to be his bedtime.

The time for denning up varies with the locality and the weather, and throughout the North-west is anywhere from November 1 to January 1. Unlike the grizzly, however, the Black Bear will often come out for a while if a warm spell follows his denning up. The Lodges note that their bears, once they are settled in their winter caves, never seem to pay any further attention to the weather. But while this is probably the rule, I have seen Black Bears out in some numbers late in December after there had been severe freezing weather during which all bears had denned up.

There is some difference of opinion as to their habits further south, and some authorities claim that at the extreme southern limit of their range the bears belonging to the Black Bear group do not hibernate at all. I incline, however, from what I have seen—or rather failed to see—to the opposite belief; for in parts of Old Mexico where, in the spring, I have seen many bears, I have again in the winter time failed to see either them or their fresh tracks, and upon making inquiry of the Indians have been told that they were asleep.

Moreover, Mr. Charles Sheldon, of New York, who for fifteen years has made a close study of bears in their natural state and has spent four years in Mexico studying bear and sheep, informs me that all the bears den up almost as early in those mountains as they do further north, and that he has never seen bears in Mexico come out of winter quarters earlier than in the United States.

There has been much scientific discussion as to the nature of this long sleep, and also much popular misconception in regard to its outward manifestations. I do not aspire to a voice in the former, but can speak from considerable experience in regard to the latter. Many, perhaps most, people seem to think that a bear that has denned up for the winter is in some mysterious, and more or less complete state of coma; that its breathing is all but suspended, and that it would be difficult, even by violence, to rouse it. They are very far from the truth. Bears sleep, but are easily roused, quick to scent danger, and ready to abandon their retreat and look up a new one if they think it necessary.

Ben, at any time during the winter, would rouse if I called him, and would even come to the mouth of his lair for a moment to greet me. I could, moreover, hear him breathing, and sometimes hear him move and readjust himself to a more comfortable position. He was a very lazy, stupid, sleepy bear; but never too stupid or sleepy to answer my call.

One fall in Washington, near Colville in the Calispell Mountains, while after deer, I noticed a strange mass of dead leaves, small sticks, pine needles, and other forest refuse gathered under the tangled trunks of a windfall, where a number of trees had been blown down crisscross. My curiosity was piqued by the queer-looking affair and I climbed along one of the tree trunks to see what it was. Suddenly, as I got almost over it, the whole mass began to shake and quiver and out came an old Black Bear and two cubs. This was the only time that I ever actually knew of a Black Bear and her cubs having denned up together. And I have never seen more than a dozen cases where it seemed probable that they had. Later on on this same trip I saw seven other Black Bear sleeping places, all in similar situations under tree trunks or tangled down-timber.

Only a year ago, up at Priest Lake, in Idaho, some friends and myself came across the tracks of a cougar, and, having gone back for dogs, we returned and put them on its trail. We were in full chase along the side of a mountain when one of the dogs attracted my attention by the way he acted. He turned aside, rushed to a dead tree that lay along the ground, and began excitedly sniffing at one end of it. I knew that the cougar could not be there and went over to see what was attracting the dog's attention, and saw instantly that a Black Bear had been denned up under the log, but, disturbed by the dog's approach, had broken out and made off down the mountain in a foot and a half of snow.

These are merely examples of many such experiences, and I have more than once followed the trail of a bear and seen where it had made itself a new retreat.

We know, since they lay up no store of provisions, that the bear does not eat during its long retirement, and although, in the north, it would be possible for it to provide itself with water by eating the snow that shuts it in, we know that bears hibernating in captivity (a thing by the way that they do not often do) neither eat nor drink.

One odd fact about the whole proceeding is that all bears of the same class in the same locality go into winter quarters and emerge from them within a few days of each other. In the Selkirk Mountains in British Columbia, I have seen where six grizzlies had broken their way through several feet of snow out of six different caves on the side of a single mountain all in one night. In localities where both species are found, the Black Bear come out from one to two months earlier than the grizzlies, and in both species the males emerge two weeks or more before the females with new cubs. But all of each kind come out within a day or two of each other.

I incline to the belief that in the majority of cases the Black Bear, when in freedom, breeds every year. Most authorities on bears who base their opinions upon observations made on captive animals, claim that both the grizzly and the Black Bear breed annually.

But a long series of observations and the closest possible attention given to this point has absolutely convinced me that it is the very rare exception when a free female grizzly breeds oftener than once in two years. I have seen many hundreds of grizzly mothers with cubs in the open, and fully as many of them were followed by yearling cubs as by spring cubs. But although (the Black Bear being much more numerous than the grizzly) I have seen many more Black Bears with cubs than grizzlies with cubs, I have never seen more than a dozen Black Bear mothers followed by yearling cubs.

I have therefore been forced to conclude that it is the habit of the Black Bear to wean its cubs and abandon them before denning up the first fall. In the case of the grizzly the mother and the cubs den up together the fall following the latter's birth, and run together during the following summer, and it is not until late in the second season that the mother turns the cubs adrift to shift for themselves. This family of young grizzlies then usually den up together and continue to run together the third summer, at the close of which the litter disbands and the individuals belonging to it take up their separate lives. I have also seen a few litters of yearling Black Bears still running in company without their mother; but as this is by no means a common sight, I believe that ordinarily Black Bear cubs den up separately after they leave their mother at the close of their first summer.

Inasmuch, however, as I have seen a few Black Bear mothers followed by yearling cubs, I assume that in these cases the mother and cubs had denned up together in the same manner that the grizzlies habitually do. And I once actually found an old Black Bear and two cubs so settled for the winter. I have also tracked an old grizzly and her cubs to where they had gone into winter quarters together, and have seen where a grizzly mother and her year-old family had emerged from hibernation in company the second spring. I have also often seen where a litter of two-year-old grizzly cubs had wintered together in one cave after leaving their mother in their third fall, but I have never seen any actual evidence of young Black Bears wintering together in this manner.

I believe that the explanation of this very striking difference of habit between the Black and the grizzly bears in the matter of breeding annually or biennially, is to be found in their different degrees of fierceness, and in the resulting fact that the Black Bear cubs are not so long in danger from the evil tempers and blood-thirsty dispositions of the grown males of their kind.

A new-born cub of either species would be instantly killed, and probably eaten, by any old male that got the opportunity; and, unnatural as this seems to us, it is true of many or most carnivorous, or partly carnivorous, animals. It is true of rats, as most boys who have bred white rats have had occasion to discover. The memory of the habit, at least, survives in the fierceness with which even a pet dog with puppies will keep the father of them away from her basket. In all zoological gardens it is necessary to separate the male bears from the female at and after the birth of cubs, and the habits of mother bears in the woods show that their instincts warn them very effectually of the wisdom of this course.

But while the Black Bear mother shows no great concern for the safety of her cubs after they have reached the age of five or six months, the grizzly mother continues, with good reason, to evade or resent the approach of other members of her tribe till well into the second year. I have on two different occasions known of a male grizzly's killing and eating a cub that had been left fastened by a chain near a camp; and in one instance I came upon a grizzly that had just killed a female and had eaten her two cubs. She had been caught in a steel trap set by a trapper, and her two cubs were with her. The male, finding her in this predicament, had doubtless attacked the cubs, and when, hampered as she was by the trap and clog, she had attempted to defend them, he had killed her too.

A female grizzly with young is one of the most dangerous animals in the world. She will allow no other bear of either sex to approach either her or them. And this invariable attitude of her fully accounts, to my mind, for her failure to breed while the young are still with her. But the Black Bear mother is not only a comparatively inoffensive animal at all times, but she seems to have no such lasting distrust of other members of her own species. I have often seen an old Black Bear asleep in the branches of a tree with her five or six-months-old cubs frisking around on the ground, when she must have been well aware that there were Black Bears of the opposite sex in the neighborhood. This is not to be put down to indifference on her part. It simply means that the necessity for watchfulness has passed. It therefore becomes easily understandable that the Black Bear mother can afford, without risk to her half-grown cubs, to breed every year in the open; while the grizzly does not, until her young are fully able to take care of themselves unaided, dare to associate with their possible enemies—the cantankerous males of the tribe.

The records of the Lodges contain one or two interesting notes relating to these matters. The first time that their original pair of Black Bears bred they did not separate the mother and father, and the first intimation that they had of the birth of cubs was the appearance of the father at the mouth of the den with a dead cub in its mouth. After that they took care to give the female separate quarters. Again, the only two occasions during the last sixteen or eighteen years on which this female has failed to breed have been in years when her cubs were allowed to remain with her throughout the summer, and when, as the owners state, she was so taken up with them that she refused to have anything to do with her mate.

This is exactly the attitude that my observations have led me to assume as habitual on the part of the free grizzly. And I imagine that the Black Bear mother adopted it in this case because, in the narrow quarters of a twenty-foot bear-pit, she was afraid to relax her vigilance, as she doubtless would have felt justified in doing in her natural surroundings.

Another point of difference between the two species that agrees with the earlier abandonment of its young by the Black Bear is the fact that these appear to breed at least a year earlier than the young of the grizzly. The latter, as we have seen, only separate and den up individually at the end of their third summer and breed the following year at the earliest; but I have seen Black Bear mothers that could not have weighed over a hundred pounds, and that made the most amusing and appealing picture of youthful responsibility.

There is a widespread notion that bears are given to travelling in company; that they are sociable animals, and that bear families—father, mother, and children—are not only to be met with in the woods, but den up together for the winter. This is not true. Only mothers and cubs or occasionally half-grown cubs of one litter ever travel together. I have never seen the slightest evidence that grown bears, male and female, ever travel in couples, even in the mating season; and I have never known a case where full-grown animals of any bear species denned up together. These statements apply no less to the Black Bear than to the grizzly.

Another point on which there is much popular misconception and disbelief is the extreme smallness of bear cubs at birth. This, at first glance, is not only astonishing, but to many people seems almost incredible. "How is it possible," they ask, "and why is it advantageous for an animal as large as a bear to have young so small? Why, the puppies of a forty-pound dog are as large as the cubs of the four-hundred pound bear!" Yet the fact remains, and in the case of the grizzly, where the mother sometimes weighs twice as much as the Black Bear mother, the cubs are, if anything, a trifle smaller at birth on the average. I have never heard the matter explained, but it seems to me that when we consider the yearly habits of the bear they tend to suggest how this peculiar race-habit was developed. A dog mother with three or four puppies, weighing six or eight ounces apiece at birth, will eat three huge meals a day and grow thin as a rail nursing her hungry youngsters. What, then, would become of a bear mother who had to nurse three or four cubs for six weeks or two months, with never a meal at all, if the cubs were born weighing five or six pounds? It looks very much as though Nature, with her usual skill at making both ends meet, had so arranged matters in the bear family that, as these animals developed the hibernating habit, the size of the cubs was reduced in proportion to the reduced ability of the mother to nourish them. And that three or four eight-ounce cubs do not make any undue demands on the resources of a three-hundred or four-hundred-pound mother is proved by the fact that both she and they are normally in excellent condition when they first come out in the spring.

FOOD AND FEEDING

The Black Bear is described as omnivorous. Literally, that means that he eats everything; and this comes pretty near to being literally true, for he has democratic tastes, a magnificent appetite, and nothing much to do between meals. Technically, however, the term means that the Black Bear is both carnivorous and herbivorous; that he eats flesh like a wolf, grass like an ox, fish like an otter, carrion like a coyote, bugs like a hen, and berries like a bird. In short he eats pretty much everything he can get, and pretty generally all he can get of it.

One would naturally imagine that so thorough-going a feeder would emerge from his long and complete winter fast ravenously hungry and ready to fall tooth and claw upon a hearty breakfast. But this is not so. Indeed, when we stop to think of it, we can see that even a bear's cast-iron constitution and digestive apparatus would hardly stand such treatment. I have examined the stomach and intestines of a bear killed just as it came out in the spring, and not only found them utterly empty, but flattened with disuse. These organs have, therefore, to be treated with consideration and coaxed back gradually to the performance of their accustomed functions. Shipwrecked sailors, rescued at the point of starvation, have to be forced by their friends to go slowly until their stomachs again get the habit of digestion; and while bears have no friends to do them a like service, they have practised long fasting for so many generations that they have developed instincts that serve the purpose.

When they first come out of the winter's den they wander around for a day or so showing little or no inclination for food. Then they make their way down to where the snow is gone and the early vegetation has begun to sprout, and eat sparingly of the tender grass shoots. But their appetites are not long in returning. By the end of a week the old saying, "hungry as a bear," is more than justified and they start in in earnest to make up for lost time. At this season they are especially fond of the parsnip-like roots of the skunk cabbage, and I have seen marshy bottom lands so dug over by bears in search of this dainty that they had almost the appearance of having been ploughed.

Here again the experience of the Lodges with their captive bears exactly confirms my own observations in the open. Mr. William R. Lodge writes me that, "When they first come out they are not hungry, and the first day or two only partake of a bite or two of parsnip or similar food that we always provide and that seems to be their most satisfactory diet after they acquire the habit of eating again." Later on these Cuyahoga Falls animals are given young dandelion leaves, clover, scraps from the hotel tables, berries, watermelons, sweet corn, and acorns. I have no doubt that this diet, so carefully approximated to the natural food of the animal in its free state, has had much to do with the success of the owners in inducing them to breed.

Wild white clover is another favorite dish of the Black Bear, and they eat the buds of the young maple shrubs and other tender green stuff. They do not, however, do nearly so much digging as the grizzly. I have seen acres of stony ground literally spaded up by the latter in search of the bulbs of the dog-tooth violet and the spring beauty. But it is only here and there, where a thin layer of earth covers a smooth hillside or ledge of rock and supports a meagre crop of small roots, that the Black Bear will scoop these up and eat them; and apart from the easy work of turning over the soft swamp earth for skunk-cabbage roots they are little given to such systematic labor.

Here indeed one sees one of the most striking differences of habit and disposition between the Black Bear and the grizzly. The grizzlies work for their food like industrious men. The Black Bear will work hard at any kind of mischief, but seems to hate to work steadily for business purposes. The grizzly will dig for hours and heap out cartloads of earth and rock to get at a nest of marmots or ground-squirrels. The Black Bear may show an interest in a marmot burrow and do a little half-hearted scratching near the entrance, but never digs deep or long for them. As far as I have ever seen, they kill nothing larger, in the way of small game, than fieldmice and such small fry. But they are both quick and clever at catching these. They will turn over stumps and roll logs aside and up-end flat stones and catch an escaping mouse before it goes a yard.

Frogs and toads are also favorite tidbits of theirs and they spend much time looking for them. They will walk along the edge of small streams and pin down a jumping frog with their lightning-quick paws; and I have seen one, when a frog escaped it and jumped into the creek, jump after it and land like a stone from a catapult, splashing water for twenty feet.

Practically nothing in the insect line comes amiss to them. They are everlastingly poking and pulling at rotten logs, old stumps, loose stones, and decaying trees, looking for caterpillars, squash-bugs, grubs, centipedes, and larvæ. Their sense of smell is wonderfully acute and one can hear them sniffing and snuffing over the punky mass of an old tree trunk they have ripped open, searching with their noses for crawling goodies.

Like all bears they are extravagantly fond of ants, and they are not only experts in finding them, but know how to take advantage of the habits of the various kinds in order to catch them. Their greatest feasts in this line are obtained when they discover the huge low hills of what, in the West, are called Vinegar Ants. These are only moderate in size, but are extremely vicious. They get their name from a strong odor, resembling that of vinegar, that they exhale when aroused. They build large hills, sometimes several feet in diameter, made up for the most part of pine needles, bits of wood, pellets of earth, and such like stuff. They are red and black in color, have powerful jaws, and rush by the thousand to give battle to any intruder that disturbs their home. It is this latter trait that makes them an easy prey to the Black Bear. When he discovers an anthill belonging to this species he walks up to it, runs one of his forelegs deep down into the inside of it, gives a turn to his paw that effectually stirs things up below, and then stretches himself out at ease to await results, with his front legs extended to the base of the hill.

Out rush the ants by companies and regiments and brigades; mad as hornets, brave as lions, smelling like a spoiled vinegar mill, and looking for trouble. They get it, almost immediately. They discover the bear's furry paws and, struggling and tumbling in the hair like angry and hurrying warriors in a jungle, they begin to swarm over them. And as fast as they come the bear licks them up. When the excitement dies down, he gives the inside of the hill another poke. This results in another sortie of defenders, and when these have stormed the hairy heights and been eaten for their pains, he repeats the operation. I believe a bear would eat a solid bushel of these insects at a sitting. On the other hand, a bear will by no means despise a single ant, and one of the best ways of making friends with a young cub is to catch a stray ant and offer it to him. He will lean forward, sniff at your fingers, and then grab the dainty as eagerly as though it weighed a pound.

There is another variety of ants, larger than the so-called Vinegar Ants, which are black and live, for the most part, under flat rocks. These the bear will lap up with his tongue after uncovering their retreat. And there is still another variety of huge black ants that nest about the roots of trees and spend their time exploring the bark and branches. I have seen them sixty feet above ground busily pursuing their affairs. Of these, too, the Black Bear is fond, and one sees him snuffing and smelling around the cracks in old trees in hopes of locating a colony of them. I have seen where bears have scratched and gnawed at the edges of a narrow opening in the lower trunk of a decaying tree, in a vain endeavor to get into the open heart of it; and again, where they had ripped off a rotting slab and gained a feast. For in cold weather these ants gather in sluggish masses and later even freeze solid—I have seen what would make a quart of them so frozen—and seem to take no harm from the cold storage. By the way, the bear is not alone in liking this peculiar diet. I have seen French Canadian lumber jacks pick up handfuls of these frozen black ants and eat them. One of them once informed me that they tasted "just the same like raspberries."

The Black Bear is also fond of bumblebees, yellow-jackets, wasps, and hornets. He is the bear that is, when occasion offers, the honeyeater; but in the Rockies and Western coast ranges there are few wild honey-bees, and so his taste in that direction is seldom indulged, but he makes up for this by hunting out and eating such bees as he can find. He will dig up bumblebees and eat them and will lap yellow-jackets off his fur exactly as he does ants. Of course the bear is fully protected by his thick coat from any attack by the bees, and if the latter sting his mouth or tongue as he swallows them, he manages to disguise the fact very thoroughly. I have never seen one shake his head or otherwise advertise a mishap of this kind.

But all these bugs and bees and ants and mice are, after all, but the luxuries and dessert of the Black Bear's diet. He is, for the most part, a vegetarian, does far more grazing than is ordinarily supposed, and has his real season of plenty and stuffing when the berry season arrives. He will travel miles to get to a berry patch, and even when tamed and half domesticated will often try to escape to the open for this annual feast. A chain that has proved amply strong enough to hold a Black Bear captive during the spring and early summer is very likely to turn up broken when the blueberries ripen. Their favorites everywhere are blueberries and huckleberries, and the black and red haws, called thornapples in New England. The sarvis berry is another of their staples. They will reach up one paw, draw down a laden berry bush, and grasping it between their forefeet will rake the fruit into their open mouths. But the Black Bear is less particular in regard to berries than the grizzly. He will eat pretty much anything in that line, even feeding on the Oregon grape in the Rockies, a food disdained by the grizzly.

In the East they also feed greedily on acorns and beechnuts, and in the West they eat the seeds that drop out of the pine cones. In the higher ranges of the Tetons and Bitter Roots, and indeed throughout the Rockies down into Mexico, there is a tree locally called the Jack Pine that bears a curious cone two or three inches across the butt and only two or three inches in depth—as broad as it is long, in fact. These cones contain very large and meaty seeds and the Black Bear is very fond of them. The Indians also cook and eat the young cones of the Jack Pine.

In addition to this the Black Bear has a great habit of peeling the bark off of balsam and of Jack Pine saplings, and of lapping the juices and gum from the wounds. They also scrape the gummy pulp from the inside of the bark and eat it. The grizzly never does these things. This pulp, however, is used by some of the Indians, who make a kind of bread out of it.

The Black Bear is fond of fish, but here again shows himself less clever and less industrious than the grizzly, who is an expert fisherman. On the Pacific slope of the Rocky Mountains almost every stream has, or used to have, its runs of salmon, these fish making their way to the upper reaches of the smaller rivers for the purpose of spawning. There are several varieties of these fish, and they enter the river and start on their long, up-hill journeys at different seasons. But one and all they are moved by a single desire—to get as far up stream as it is possible to go; and are driven forward by so strong an instinct that neither wounds, nor weariness, nor exhaustion, nor the fear of death itself, deters them from attempting (and sometimes accomplishing) what seems like the impossible.

They come from undiscovered regions of the sea in uncountable billions. In untold millions they enter the mouths of the great rivers. They turn off into each tributary stream by hundreds of thousands. They fill the tributaries of these tributaries. And finally one finds them, still in their hundreds, filling the pools of the smaller rivers, leaping, floundering, all but crawling through the riffles and shallows of the smaller creeks, thousands of feet above the sea, and still undaunted. And few of the invading millions ever find their way back to the ocean from which they came. From the moment that they enter the mouths of the larger rivers, every living creature, from man downward, begins to take toll of them. Those that pass the nets and salmon wheels of the canning factories, that elude the talons of the eagles and ospreys, that are missed by the paws of the bears and the cougars, the teeth of the otters and the mink, arrive at the headwaters of their selected stream in a pitiable condition of wounds and exhaustion. Their fins are nothing but bare spines. Their sides are torn by rocks, they are thin from fasting, and when they have deposited and fertilized the eggs that they have come so far to find fit hatcheries for, they are, for the most part, utterly unable to manage the long return journey. Then they fall an easy prey to any animal that finds them. And many animals gather to the feast. Here is the free-lunch counter of the wilderness; during the salmon runs everything in the mountains lives on fish: bears, cougars, coyotes, wolverines, lynx; in Alaska the very geese gorge themselves on salmon; and the Black Bear gets his share of the loot.

The grizzly, as I have said, is an expert fisherman. I have seen one toss out seventeen big salmon in less than an hour, and after eating his fill bury the rest of his catch for future use. But the Black Bears only fish on their own account occasionally and in very shallow water. They will wander along the trails on the banks of the small streams, and if salmon are struggling over the riffles, will jump in and catch one or two. But they are too much lacking in patience to wait for the fish as the grizzly does, and too improvident to do more than supply the need of the moment when the opportunity comes unwaited for. And they are quite satisfied, for the most part, to take the leavings of others or to feed on stranded or dead fish. They often get crumbs from the table of the golden eagle, the bald eagle, and the osprey; and sometimes, when one of these birds catches a fish too heavy to fly away with, a Black Bear will drive the fisherman away and eat his catch for him.

But we began by saying that the Black Bear was in part carnivorous, and so far, we have not justified the claim by anything more fleshy than a field-mouse. The truth is that the Black Bear much prefers to have his meat "well hung," as some sportsmen express it. That is to say, he really prefers carrion. Any kind of a carcass makes a strong appeal to him, and I do not believe that meat can be too putrid to suit his taste. Ben, when he was out walking with me during the time we lived in Missoula, would turn aside to sniff over any dead cat or hen that he came across—even if nothing remained of it but dried skin and bones. And he would actually lie down and roll on the find, and, if allowed, would then pick it up in his mouth and carry it home for a nest egg.

But in spite of his preference for carrion, the Black Bear soon learns to take advantage of easily procurable live meat. They are remarkably adaptable animals, take kindly to civilization, and accommodate themselves readily to the conditions and opportunities that follow in its wake. They very soon realize it if they are free from interference, and will, with the slightest encouragement, begin to impose upon you. They will live under your barn with the best will in the world. And they'll learn to steal sheep. In some localities they get to be a serious nuisance in this way. But their favorite civilized dish is young pig. In some regions the ranchmen in the spring turn their hogs out into swamps to feed on the roots of the skunk cabbage; but if Black Bears happen to be plentiful in the neighborhood they are very likely to get not only the skunk cabbage but the pigs as well. There appears to be something about a shoat that appeals directly to the Black Bear instinct. They learn to be sheep thieves; but they appear to be born pig thieves. The summer that I caught Ben, as we were returning to Spokane across the Palouse farming country, we stopped at a ranch overnight and left Ben tied under a small shed while we unpacked and stabled our horses. It happened that there was an old sow with a litter of young pigs in a pen at the rear end of the shed, and that there was a hole in the pen for the young ones to come and go by. And when we came back to get Ben we found him lying by this hole with one paw stuck through it, waiting for a pig. And just as we arrived he actually slapped one on the nose and almost caught it. And he was only a little larger than the pig himself.

Of course the diet of the Black Bear, like that of the grizzly, and of most other wild animals, depends largely upon the locality in which they live. There are regions where, of necessity, the bear are largely if not altogether vegetarians; and others where, at certain seasons, they live almost wholly upon fish or largely upon carrion. It is never safe to generalize from localized observations as to the food habits of any animal, and it is only very carefully and as the result of a broad experience that one should venture to ascribe to any species the traits that one has observed in individuals. There is one feeding habit of the Black Bear, however, that I believe to be universally typical. They never make caches of food. The grizzlies will, as I have already said, bury the fish they cannot eat for future use. They will also drag away and bury or hide the carcass of any animal they have found and will return to feed on it until it is all consumed; or they will carefully cover it where it lies with earth and leaves and branches to prevent other animals from finding it in their absence. The Black Bear does not look so far ahead. He will carry away a few pounds of meat or bones in his mouth, but beyond that appears to take no thought for the morrow. When he has sated his appetite on a carcass he will leave it where and as he found it. He lives from hand to mouth and is the Happy Hooligan of the woods.

Sources

Grinnell, George Bird. "The Solitary Hunter." *Beyond the Old Frontier Adventures of Indian-Fighters, Hunters, and Fur-Traders.* New York: Scribner's, 1913.

McCracken, Harold. "The Alaska Grizzly." *Field and Stream*, 1920.

Mills, Enos A. "The Grizzly: Our Greatest Wild Animal." In *The Grizzly: Our Greatest Wild Animal.* Charleston, SC: CreateSpace Independent Publishing Platform.

Mueller, Larry, and Marguerite Reiss. "Tundra Terror." In *Bear Attacks of the Century: True Stories of Courage and Survival*, 81–88. Guilford, CT: Lyons Press, 2024.

Reid, Captain Mayne. "A Bear Trap Gone Wrong." *A Hunter's Feast: or, Conversations around the Camp Fire.* Project Gutenberg ebook, 2007.

Roosevelt, Theodore. "The Black Bear." *Hunting the Grisly and Other Sketches*, 10–13. New York: G. P. Putnam's Sons, 1902 (originally published in 1893).

———. "Hunting the 'Grisly.'" *Hunting the Grisly and Other Sketches*, 24–37. New York: G. P. Putnam's Sons, 1902 (originally published in 1893).

Snow, Kathleen. "Horror in Yellowstone." In *Taken by Bear in Yellowstone: More than a Century of Harrowing Encounters between Grizzlies and Humans.* Guilford, CT: Lyons Press, 2016.

———. "The Grizzly on the Elk Mountain Trail." In *Taken by Bear in Glacier National Park: Harrowing Encounters between Grizzlies and Humans.* Guilford, CT: Lyons Press, 2020. Reprinted by permission of Lyons Press.

Underwood, Lamar. "On Dangerous Ground." In *On Dangerous Ground.* New York: Doubleday, 1989. Reprinted by permission.

———. "Grizzly Attack Survival Epic." *American Frontiersman.* Reprinted by permission of Lamar Underwood.

Wright, William H. "The Happy Hooligan." *The Black Bear*, 105–116. New York: Charles Scribner's Sons, 1910.

Index

acorns, 252
Adams, James Capen, 79
Adirondacks, 159, 167
Africa, 121, 159
African Game Trails (Roosevelt), 121
Air Force, United States, 112, 118
Alaska, 254; Anchorage, 117; "bearcats," 181–85; Frosty Peak, 182; grizzly bears in, 83, 95–96, 101, 103–4, 106–7, 112, 137, 171–73, 178–85; King Cove, 174, 176–78; Kuparuk oil field, 111; native Alaskans, 111–12, 181, 182, 184; Oliktok Point radar site, 111–18; Point Lay radar, 112; polar bears in, 111–17; Prudhoe Bay, 112; Toubok River, 89–107; wind storms in, 174–77
Alaska Peninsula, 171–74, 178, 181
Alaska Peninsula brown bear (*Ursus gyas*): charging by, 173, 180–81; meat of, 181; size of, 171–73, 178, 181–85; skins, 181, 185; tracks of, 83, 181–82.

See Alaska Peninsula brown bear
Alaska Range, 97–99
Alleghenies, 159
The American Natural History (Hornaday), 79
Anchorage, Alaska, 117
antelope, 26–29, 36–37, 46, 203–5
ants, 250–51
Arikara (Ree) tribe, 194–95
Ashley, William, 193–94
Astringent Creek Bridge, Yellowstone Park, 4, 8, 14
Astringent Creek–Broad Creek Trail, Yellowstone Park, 4, 6, 9, 14
Audubon, John James, 80
Autumn Creek Trail, Glacier Park, 70

Bach, Orville E., Jr., 8
balsam bark, 253
Basel, Switzerland, 3
Bates (Captain), 142–43
Bear Attacks (Herrero), 20, 229
bear attacks, bears and. *See specific topics*